HANDBOOK FOR ART AND DESIGN STUDENTS

HANDBOOK FOR ART AND DESIGN STUDENTS

ROBIN JESSON
Head of the Faculty of Art and Design, Barnet College

Longman   London and New York

Longman Group Limited
Longman House, Burnt Mill, Harlow
Essex CM20 2JE, England
Associated companies throughout the world

Published in the United States of America
by Longman Inc., New York
© Longman Group Limited 1984

First published 1984

British Library Cataloguing in Publication Data
Jesson, Robin
  Handbook for art and design students. –
  (Longman art and design series)
  1. Arts – Study and teaching – Grant
  Britain
  I. Title
  700'.7104   NX343

  ISBN 0-582-41294.3

Set in 10/11pt Linotron 202 Plantin
Printed in Hong Kong by
Commonwealth Printing Press Ltd

For Christopher and Kate

Contents

Acknowledgements

We are indebted to the following for permission to reproduce copyright material:

Council for National Academic Awards for extracts from *Directory of Degree & Diploma of Higher Education Courses* 1981–2; Kodak Ltd for Table & adapted extracts from pp 19, 6–8, 15 *Kodak Publication No AM2–1(H)*; Regional Advisory Council for Technological Education for adapted Table from p 102/3 *A Compendium of Advanced Courses in Colleges of Further & Higher* Education; Technician Educational Council for an extract from Section 3 *General Guidelines for Art & Design Studies* pub. Apr. 1979; the Victoria and Albert Museum for our Figs. 1.6, 1.7, 1.8, 1.9 and 1.12; Peter Blake for our Fig. 1.11; the Institute of Agricultural History and Museum of English Rural Life for our Fig. 3.2; Ironbridge Gorge Museum Trust for our Fig. 3.5.

Special thanks are due to the following artists, designers, lecturers and institutions for their expert advice on the specialist design areas dealt with in this handbook:

Browen Buckley – Fashion design
Roger Butler – Ceramics and drawing systems
Susan Clark – Print-making
Steven Davis – Textiles
Stephanie Dobson – Jewellery and silversmithing
Peter Henley – Art and design materials
International Wool Secretariat – Textiles
Charles Marriott – Drawing
John Marsh – Graphic design
Brian Newman – Drawing systems
Mardi Ross – Textiles
Francis Sharp – International Institute for Cotton – Textiles
William Townsend – Drawing
Cathleen Ward – Fashion illustration
Roy Wickens – Drawing systems

Introduction

You should be able to pick up a piece of wood and find you have a bird in your hand.

Pablo Picasso

This is a reference book and consumer guide for the beginner. It contains basic information on the nature of various creative activities, materials, equipment, research facilities, college courses and career prospects.

Many art and design activities such as ceramics, jewellery, photography, weaving, print-making, machine-knitting, fashion design and textile design and printing can be inexpensively carried out by beginners with the minimum of facilities. Full-time and part-time courses in departments, faculties and colleges of art and design provide access to more sophisticated resources and to teaching by professional artists and designers.

The practice of art and design involves the development of perceptual, conceptual, intuitive, imaginative and analytical abilities involving problem-solving; a knowledge and understanding of social, historical and environmental influences; skill acquisition; the learning of a specialised vocabulary and the development of individual talents.

CREATIVITY

At the beginning of all creative work the individual response to a given situation is all that exists. It is this response that stimulates in the creative personality the activities that follow. It can be nurtured and cultivated, but it is almost impossible to teach and cannot be learnt by reading a book. The only practical method is to attempt creative work.

Some people are inhibited from trying to learn a craft or involving themselves in creative activities because they believe that they cannot draw. In fact, most people from an early age can make marks on a surface which quite clearly represent their view of the visible world or that of their imagination. What concerns them, however, is their belief, usually gained as they approach adult life, that they cannot draw when comparing their efforts with the drawing abilities of those they admire. Everyone can draw, but some can more easily communicate by drawing than in other ways such as by the written word, music or speech. What is communicated is more important than how it is communicated. It is possible to train someone to observe and record visual observations. This involves a process of selection, from all the data available, of the most important elements. This selection process is unique for each person and it is the quality of what is communicated that determines whether or not the selection has been appropriate.

DEVELOPMENT OF IDEAS

Everyone concerned with the creative process has to start with an idea that can be developed, usually progressively, until the potential of the original idea is exhausted. This ability to develop an idea beyond the initial stages is crucial to the development of the artist and designer. The inherent possibilities contained within the original thought must be discovered, drawn out, explored and experimented with, using a range of materials. Without this development only repetition can follow; tired, outworn cliches which lack creative vitality. A simple example will help to explain some possibilities for the development of ideas.

An observation of the changing effects of light on a group of objects can start with a series of monochrome studies, perhaps in pencil, develop into tonal studies in colour and lead to work in a variety of media, possibly including photography, print-making and designs carried out in clay, metal, wood, plaster, plastics or mixed media materials. The idea could be developed into a print for textiles or for a fashion fabric, used as the basis for film animation or treated as a surface pattern on domestic tableware or household linens. This exploratory method is also a means of self-discovery, testing the individual's capability to respond to a particular problem and to exhaust all the possibilities. It is not necessary to have expensive and sophisticated tools in order to make worthwhile images. In fact, primitive tools often liberate the creative senses in unexpected ways. It is also a common experience to find that accidents or unintentional developments can be used creatively.

CONVENTIONS

Art and design have well-established conventions. A drawing such as that by the student shown in Fig. 1 uses such a convention. The model

Fig. 1   Life drawing by Foundation Course student, Faculty of Art and design – Barnet College

drawn by the student was not surrounded by a line; and a photograph of the same model would have quite a different appearance. The idea that a drawn line can represent what is actually seen in the visual world as solid form, or even that a drawing in black and white can convey the form and character of a person whose real existence is in colour is widely understood and accepted. Because artistic conventions are so well established it is possible to communicate complex and sophisticated ideas in simple and direct ways.

Another means of communication by convention is the symbol. Information signs are an example of complex instructions being conveyed in a manner which is direct and immediately intelligible. Symbols can be understood internationally and easily overcome language barriers. It is not necessary to know any language to find the way to the toilets at an airport. The stylised male and female figures shown on the signs are immediately understood, even by very small children. The map of the London Underground system is a brilliant example of a complex railway system explained in readily understandable symbolic terms. In that the designer has combined colour, signs and the names of stations to explain complex links between different lines, connections to main railway stations and the sequence of stations on each line without directly referring to the actual geography of the area.

VOCABULARY

Studying for any activity, whether as a potential professional or as an amateur, requires a basic knowledge of the vocabulary used by the practitioners. All professions have a particular way of using language, a jargon, and artists and designers use some words in ways which are not common to their meaning in everyday life. Words such as form, line, tone, mass, structure and volume also have uses in other art forms such as music and architecture. In order to communicate effectively with others it is necessary to understand this vocabulary and in order to aid understanding a glossary is included at the end of the book. Words that appear in the glossary are signalled in the text by an asterisk.

TECHNOLOGY

Rapid technological developments are affecting the work of designers as they also affect other aspects of work in general. The use of microprocessors* as design tools, the development of 'dry' camera systems, holograms* and lasers*, the use of computers for the production processes in the fashion and textile industries and the draughting capabilities of the new technology mean that young designers looking forward to a working life in art and design must be prepared to adjust and rethink the use of the tools by which creative expression is made tangible.

STYLE

Everyone sees the visual world in a different way, although individual reactions are conditioned by cultural conventions.

Avoiding a stereotyped response to a creative problem is essential. Simply repeating what was originally developed by, for example, the Art Nouveau* movement is negative. Rediscovery has a place in creativity, but it cannot be done in the terms of the past. Developments in the visual arts have parallels in literature, music, architecture and philosophical ideas, and an appreciation of these links can add new dimensions to individual responses to contemporary life. Such relationships can more easily be appreciated by a study of the past. Not all the characteristics of a particular period will come together at the same time in the same place. The style of a period is a product of action and reaction on the part of creative people and the speed by which such information is spread. The present rate of technological change and the fast dissemination of information now means that an awareness of stylistic change is rapidly spread world-wide by very large numbers of people, an international style. The time-gap between the development of an idea and its assimilation into the broader area of style can now be just a few months. This particularly applies to the more ephemeral arts: fashion, graphic design, television, film and photography. Economics can also have an effect on style. This development of new materials with significant cost savings can be reflected in the style of furniture or the manufacture of carpets or textiles. The speeding up of the information process can lead to a retreat from the contemporary scene into the styles of the past, such as Victoriana or the period of the 1920s and 1930s. The speed of change, with its economic implications, can inhibit people from living directly within their own time in terms of style. It is expensive to maintain a life style rapidly adapting to stylistic changes and a retreat into the past is an easy escape. Some people possibly consider it better to be completely out of date than always just out of date, and it is often fashionable to live in the style of the past rather than the present.

Finding the best means for developing creative ideas and the kind of support that is available is the aim of this book. Some of the illustrations are by young art and design students at the start of their professional careers. All the recommendations for materials and equipment are based on the practical experience of artists and designers who are also teachers.

Note

This Handbook contains references to materials and equipment from a number of manufacturers and agents. While every effort has been made to ensure that the products mentioned are available, readers are advised to check with their local suppliers as some items may be withdrawn and manufacturers are continually improving and modifying their products.

CHAPTER 1

General art and design

1.1 DRAWING

Drawing is a fundamental art and design activity concerned with the visual recording of observations, the expression of concepts in visual terms and image-making.

Experience will ensure the choice of the most suitable drawing implement for the image required. It is essential to experiment with different tools and to avoid developing techniques that can inhibit the individuality of image-making. Be prepared to be surprised by some of the images made and to see them as personal ways of communication.

Drawing systems are ways of visually explaining complex ideas to other people.

1.2 DRAWING MATERIALS

Chalks

Faber-Castell make a good, square-section chalk, available in twelve colours. They are made of an anti-dust composition and paper-wrapped so that both hands may be left clean. Twelve assorted colours are ready-packed in a box.

All work in chalk requires careful fixing to prevent smudging. A suitable lacquer fixative should be obtained for this purpose (see section on fixatives).

Charcoal

The best drawing charcoal is specially prepared for artists and designers. One of the best charcoals to use is in the Pitt range of artists' materials. It is made in five grades, extra soft, soft, medium, hard and extra hard and is round in shape. Rowney make a charcoal pencil, medium grade, which is a useful addition to life-drawing materials. The Criteruim Clutch Pencil is suitable for 5–6 mm diameter leads of charcoal. The removable tip is fitted with a sharpener and supplied with a length of Conte compressed charcoal.

Crayons

It is sometimes difficult to manage the whole range of colours and tones of crayons until familiar with their characteristics. The type of working surface is very important. Normally avoid shiny, smooth surfaces which cannot give the crayon enough bite to work at its best. Gain experience with crayons of one colour in a range of tones before buying a number of different colours. Explore the water-resistant wax or oil qualities of some crayons. Use them with other mediums such as drawing inks or acrylic colours.

Crayons are available in a number of forms including crayon pencils, square and round section, water resistant and water soluble. One of the largest ranges is made by the Swiss manufacturer Caran D'Ache. Their range is available with a choice of thirty colours. Neo-colour 1 is water resistant. Neo-colour 2 is water soluble.

Crayons are suitable for use on a wide range of materials and are light resistant. It is advisable to use crayons in a special holder as this allows the utilisation of the whole length of the crayon and helps to keep the artwork free of unwanted smudges. Neo-colour 1 crayons are soluble in white spirit or turpentine and, when soluble, can be used with a brush. They can be erased by gently scraping the surface with a knife or scalpel.

Another firm that provides an interesting range of crayons is Berol. They offer three main types which are useful, including a chunky, round-section crayon called Cascade and a plastic-sheathed stick of solid colour called Verithik which can be resharpened. The colour range of both types, however, is limited. Berol's Artworker square-section crayon is, however, available in fifteen colours including black and white.

The Pitt range is ideal for life drawing. These crayons are made in black (medium and soft), white, sanguine and sepia (medium) in square sections. They also make a set of grey crayons, two each of six shades, and a set of brown crayons with twelve different assorted brown shades. One advantage of using a limited range of colours and tones is the opportunity to make contrasts by tone alone, without changing the colour.

Conte crayons are very popular. They are made in black – No. 1 medium (HB); No. 2 soft (B); and No. 3 extra soft (BB) – sepia, bistre and red sanguine in one degree only.

Erasers

Erasers can be the curse of drawing. The first inclination of many beginners is to produce a 'work of art' and this often involves rubbing out any marks that fail to achieve the desired effect.

The time could be more profitably used by actually drawing. A study of the drawings of famous artists will often show that all their errors of observation have not been erased but left as a record alongside the finished work. This particularly applies when the artists are of the stature of Leonardo or Michelangelo.

Erasers, however, have their place and for some work, where preliminary stages have to be removed, they are essential.

There are special erasers available for a number of specific tasks. The most useful types are as follows:

Plastic (kneaded putty rubber). This can be shaped, is non-abrasive and suitable for soft graphite, charcoal and pastel work.
Gum (art gum). Free of grease, soft and pliable, but crumbles so can be messy to use. Cheese-like in texture.
Blaisdell (paper covered – pencil shaped). For erasing detail. Eraser-sticks for Indian ink and ballpoint.
Ink eraser. Very hard and abrasive. Will easily scratch paper surfaces.
Plastic (vinyl). Hard – does not crumble.
Fibreglass. For very difficult erasing. Pencil or cigar shaped. Ideal for Indian ink erasing.
Erasing knives. Similar in design to a scalpel, with a specially designed blade.

For removing feltmarker inks from artwork or clothing the Edding Thinner V100 may be useful. Always experiment first on a small unimportant sample. It will not work on PVC (polyvinyl chloride) Ordinary ink marks can sometimes be removed with methylated spirit.

A useful drafting eraser is the Mars 527–30, a white vinyl eraser which comes in a pencil-shaped holder.

For erasing type or print use Tipp-Ex or a similar correction fluid. Liquid erasers sometimes need dilution with an approved solvent to maintain the flow.

Partial erasing or highlighting of texts can be effectively done with a suitable highlighter such as the Staedtler top-marker which is available in six colours.

All major manufacturers offer ranges of erasers. The Edding range is particularly useful for design students.

Feltmarkers

Feltmarkers normally consist of a barrel-shaped ink container, often short and chunky in appearance, with a felt top providing a stroke width from about 0.3 mm to 2.0 mm. Some manufacturers offer refillable markers and replacement felts. The colour range of Magic Markers is 123 colours including 18 shades of grey. Feltmarkers have some limitations for drawing, mainly due to their squat shape and the nature of the felt tip, but they are widely used by graphic designers for 'roughs', i.e. preliminary layouts.

Tips are usually chamfered, pointed, square or rectangular. Markers are available for all types of surfaces including metal, stone and wood.

The range of inks include permanent, lightfast, waterproof, opaque and water-soluble types.

The Berol range includes a refillable marker with three interchangeable nibs and a specially developed valve which acts to stop evaporation, a problem with these markers when they are not in use.

One of the largest specialist ranges is provided by C. W. Edding who were pioneers in this field. They produce seventeen different types of feltmarker ranging from those designed for drawing on unusual surfaces such as plastic foils to three made for use as writing instruments. The Edding 750 with a range of five colours, black, red, blue, green and yellow, is a good basic feltmarker for general use.

Fibrepens

Fibrepens offer more control than feltmarkers as they are usually longer in shape and the fibre tips are capable of detailed work. The stroke width varies from 0.3 mm to 3 mm, but also includes tips capable of being used as a fine brush such as the Edding 1380 brushpen. The tips can also vary from firm to supple. The fibrepen colour range is large. For some types as many as forty-eight colours are available. Rechangeable cartridges are made for some models.

Fibrepens are widely used, particularly in design studios and for fashion illustration.

Always purchase pens from a specialist retailer if possible. Edding offer twenty-one different types of fibrepens for a variety of purposes. The Staedtler Lumocolor range is designed for overhead projector work. This range is available in both non-permanent (water-soluble) and permanent (solvent-based) types.

The Edding 1380 brushpen is very popular and is available in twelve colours; but the three primary colours plus black would be a useful start to a collection.

Fixative

All work that is likely to smudge or rub off needs spraying with a lacquer fixative. It is possible to buy a small mouth spray diffuser and a bottle of fixative solution quite cheaply, but the most effective method is to use an aerosol fixative. Follow the manufacturer's instructions carefully. It is often necessary to work in a well-ventilated space as the fumes from the lacquer can cause distress. Fixatives are transparent and should not affect the appearance of the work.

Graphite sticks

Solid sticks of graphite without a wood, pencil-like casing. They can be sharpened like a pencil. Very useful for life drawing, they are made in three degrees of hardness, HB, 3B, 6B, by Faber-Castell.

Lead holders

A useful alternative to the pencil is the lead holder containing drawing lead. Holders are also sometimes known as automatic pencils and their main advantage is the ready availability of the lead for a period of continuous drawing. A wide range of holders is available and the prices vary considerably. For beginners a simple holder is quite suitable, but the more advanced holders have an almost indefinite life and are elegant, well-designed additions to a set of drawing tools. Remember that a different holder will be needed for each line width of lead, but one holder can contain leads of different degrees of hardness.

The majority of holders provide an automatic feed system which keeps the lead always available for drawing. Line widths range from 0.3 mm to 3.0 mm. The width is usually identified on the holder. Some makes include a cleaning needle and an eraser.

The Caran D'Ache Fixpencil range with a large 2 mm lead is useful for all types of drawing. The Edding P3 is made in three diameter sizes, 0.5 mm, 0.7 mm and 0.9 mm, with a choice of seven degrees of hardness. Berol make a range of four types of holder, of which the Turquoise 10 is specially designed for draughtsmen, and Faber-Castell have an excellent range called the TK with fully automatic lead feed available on the TK-Matic. The Mars range from Staedtler is also very popular. This firm makes an inexpensive fineline lead holder (0.5 mm only) called the 775 Micro F and a larger diameter 2 mm lead holder called the 785 Mars Technico. For information about leads see page 13.

Inks

Drawing inks of all kinds are widely used. The traditional Indian ink is excellent for work being prepared for reproduction and the small bottles of coloured drawing inks have many uses in the studio. They can be used with pen or brush or used in combination with Indian ink. A little ink goes a long way so only initially buy in small quantities. Brushes and pens should be thoroughly cleaned after use.

Drawing inks are useful when used with other drawing materials. Explore their water-soluble characteristics by using them with wax or oil crayons. Their staining possibilities should also be explored.

There are a wide range of ink cartridges made for refillable pens of all kinds. Jars or pots of refill inks are also useful for some feltmarkers and similar tools with a large ink storage capacity. Feltmarkers that have dried up can sometimes be used again by using an appropriate thinner such as the Edding V100. Most inks can be sprayed or used with an airbrush.

Indian inks

Pitch black, fast drying, waterproof. Available in a range of sizes from a number of manufacturers.

Drawing inks

Water-resistant and waterproof when dry. These inks are intermixable and can be usually diluted with distilled water. They dry quickly but are vulnerable to light, and therefore work needs protection if the colours are not to fade. A good colour range is available. Winsor & Newton stock a range of twenty colours, together with black and white. They also have gold and silver non-waterproof inks. Rowney has a range also of twenty colours, including black.

Choose about six colours for a start: Lemon yellow; Vermilion; French ultramarine; Brown; Black; White.

Drawing inks can be used with pens and water-colour brushes.

Instruments

Work in technical illustration, graphic design, interior design, exhibition design or other aspects of three-dimensional design may require a set of drawing instruments. Some students will already have instruments purchased while at school and in many cases these will be suitable for the early stages of college courses. Students should consult their tutors before purchasing any new instruments.

Precision drawing instruments can be very expensive as they are made for work of a highly skilled nature. Most manufacturers offer a student range of compass sets such as the Faber-Castell 72503 which includes a divider and compass with pencil and pen inserts. An adjustable triangle, set square, protractor and rule may be needed to complete a basic kit which can be extended as the need arises.

Rulers

Purchase a good-quality rule. Ideally this should show both imperial and metric graduation. Wood rules usually last longer than plastic. A long steel rule for use with a knife when cutting card is very useful, particularly when mounting completed work. A rule approximately 60 cm long is ideal for this type of work.

Knives

A basic cutting tool is essential for a variety of tasks. The most familiar type is probably the Stanley knife with a set of interchangeable blades.

Other makes include the Edding M18 cutter and the UNO Neatrim multipurpose cutter which is shaped like a pen and has a retractable blade. The cutter fits Swann Morton blades and also has a removable end for accessory storage. Surgical scalpels can also be useful general cutting tools. Buy a knife that is capable of easily cutting through thick mounting card and preferably one with interchangeable blades.

All knives can be dangerous if used incorrectly and many minor accidents to fingers occur when work in the studio has to be mounted. Never draw the blade towards the body and always use a suitable support underneath the work to avoid cutting other surfaces. Use a cutting mat if one is available.

Palette knives

These knives are available in steel and stainless steel. The straight-blade knives range in length from about 75 mm to 130 mm (3 in to 5 in). The trowel knives are made in a range of shapes including diamond, pear and trowel. For work with acrylic or polymer paints a stainless steel knife is essential. Use a knife to mix the paint on the palette and to apply paint when an impasto (thick laying on of pigments) is required. Beginners can usually manage with one straight blade and one trowel.

Leads

All leads have to be used with some type of lead holder (see page 11). They are graded by line width and hardness. Line widths range from 0.3 mm to 3 mm. Leads are available in black and ranges of up to twenty-one colours for use on a variety of surfaces.

There are two main types of leads: graphite, which is a mixture of graphite and clay, extruded and baked; and polymer, which has a polymer resin base.

The whole range of leads are not needed by beginners and the number of line widths purchased will depend on the number of lead holders available. Users of lead holders and leads are likely initially to need about four line widths in the 6H to 6B hardness range. The softer the lead the larger the diameter/line width.

Pastels

Pastels are pigments ground with chalk, clay and other ingredients, bound with gum and manufactured in sticks. A large range of colours is available.

The Faber-Castell Polychromos range is made in 72 shades and Rowney's Artists' Soft Pastels in 193 colours including blacks and whites.

Pastels are fragile and softer than crayons, but this characteristic produces their distinctive effect. Pastel work must be fixed with a suitable fixative.

It is well worth experimenting with all types of media, but it is unlikely that beginners will need more than a representative range of pastels. A set of twelve pastels from grey to black (Rowney Tonal Selection) is a good introduction to this medium. Also recommended is the set of twelve assorted colours made by Conte – bistre, black, dark green, dark ultramarine, light blue, orange, pink, red, St Michael green, white, yellow and yellow ochre.

Pencils

The most familiar drawing instrument is the black graphite pencil. The lead pencil is really made from a form of carbon called graphite. This is mixed with clay, extruded and baked in special kilns. The degree of hardness of the finished lead varies according to the proportions of clay used in this process. Figure 1.1 shows a pencil drawing.

The hardness of the lead is measured on a scale from 9B (very black and very soft) to 9H (very hard). HB (hard black) is approximately in the centre of the range. The softer the lead the more dense the tone it will produce. The effect of the lead also varies according to the type of drawing surface that is used. The smoother the surface the more even will appear the areas of tone.

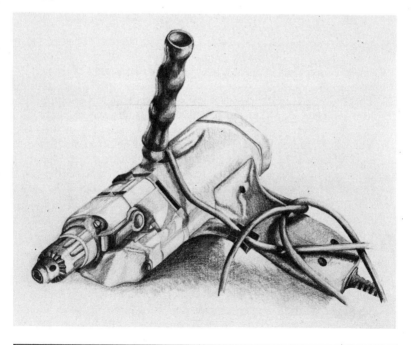

Fig. 1.1   Pencil Drawing by Foundation Course student, Faculty of Art & Design, Barnet College

A pencil is a very subtle and sophisticated tool capable of a wide variety of effects and there is a very large choice of pencils on the market. There are coloured pencils in ranges of up to sixty colours and water-soluble, spirit-soluble, indelible and special-purpose pencils for a wide number of uses. Faber-Castell make useful life-drawing pencils in their Pitt range. These have a thick core and are made in three grades – soft, medium and hard. They also make a sanguine, sepia and white crayon version. Many beginners like the Black Beauty pencils which are available in round and hexagonal shapes. These extra thick, black pencils are equivalent to hardness grade 4B. The black-lead Castell range has one of the largest gradings available from one manufacturer, from 8B to 9H. Berol, another major pencil manufacturer make ten types of pencil ranging from their Venus Drawing, available in fourteen degrees of hardness from 6B to 6H, to their Alphex pencil, a large-diameter, hexagonal pencil with a dense, soft black lead very useful for large bold drawings. The Mars–Lumograph range also offers nineteen degrees of hardness. Staedtler also makes the Tradition and Noris ranges with a more limited range of hardness.

Chinagraph pencils are specially made for marking polished surfaces including glass, acetate, china and film. The marks are impervious to water. The Royal Sovereign range has six colours and white.

Coloured pencils are made in large colour ranges. Polychromos pencils have a range of sixty colours and are soluble in white spirit. They include an excellent range of grey shades. Another very good range of colours is made by Rexel and called the Derwent. This firm has a choice of seventy-two colours in either pencil form or as 8 mm square blocks. Pencils and blocks can be purchased in sets and the pencils are colour tipped for easy identification.

Choosing a pencil from the range in a specialist retailers is really a matter of personal preference. Because pencils are cheap and easily obtainable they often get mislaid or borrowed, perhaps never to be found or returned. The tendency, therefore, is to buy more pencils than are really needed. The degree of hardness between grades is worth recording in a notebook. Make a 'grade' chart, small areas of tone representing all the grades, leaving gaps for the ones yet to be purchased. Never let pencils get too short so that control is lost over the marks they make. Get a pencil lengthener which will extend the pencil and its effective life. Always keep pencils sharp, literally razor sharp, by using only very sharp blades for sharpening.

A selection of about six pencils will be useful for general drawing. Try a 6B, 4B, 3B, 2B, H and a 2H.

Pens

It is important to be familiar with the different types of pens available for the artist and designer and be aware of the tasks they are designed to perform. Buy a specialist pen if it is required for the work that is to be done. There are pens for calligraphy, lettering, technical drawing of all kinds, mapping, drawing on film, drafting, computing, plotting and many other categories.

Technical drawing pens

There are several types of precision technical drawing pens. These pens are sophisticated drawing instruments, expensive and requiring careful upkeep if they are to function efficiently. Some manufacturers make special ranges of pens for students. The main characteristics of technical drawing pens are the steel point used for drawing and the rechargeable, automatic ink feed which enables the pen to be constantly ready for use. The pen should not leak and the ink should flow easily and evenly.

Pens are sold either individually or, more usually, in sets comprising a number of pens capable of alternative line thickness. Some sets also include technical drawing instruments. The choice of line widths ranges from about 0.1 mm. to 2.0 mm. Interchangeable points allow for changes of line width, but if more than one line width is regularly used it makes sense to have more than one pen.

When coated drawing film is used the pen should be fitted with a tungsten carbide point as the normal stainless steel points are affected by this type of surface.

A technical drawing pen is something of a long-term investment. Design students have found the Marsmatic 700 trouble free and easy to handle. It is available in nine line widths, but it is unlikely that any beginner would need the complete set.

Ruling pens

These are one of the simplest forms of ink drawing pen. They are, however, sometimes difficult for the beginner to handle. Ruling-pen points are available for attaching to compasses.

Gillott's pens, with a wide range of nibs and different types of ink reservoirs are recommended for calligraphy, lettering and other graphic work. William Mitchell's pens are ideal for calligraphy.

1.3 DRAWING SYSTEMS

The visual world is normally seen through two eyes. This is called binocular vision. Because each eye sees a slightly different view of the world it is possible to judge distances and assess relationships in sizes. However, when information from both eyes has to be drawn on a flat surface, a picture plane, it is sometimes necessary to use a device called perspective if the final result is to give an illusion of the space that exists in reality.

Perspective

Perspective assumes one point of view, as if the world were seen with one eye closed. In order to draw 'in perspective' it may be necessary to first establish an eye level, an imaginary horizontal line across the picture plane representing the horizon. The higher the line, the greater the depth of the foreground, that is, the space in front of the 'horizon'. The angle at which any receding objects are viewed in relation to the eye level will change and the effect of this is to make identical objects appear to change in size as they recede, even over a very small distance. The apparent differences in size are exaggerated by the angles at which they are seen. The fixing of a 'horizon' can also determine whether receding diagonal lines slope upwards or downwards towards the point where they appear to meet, known as the vanishing point, which need not, however, be within the picture plane.

Horizontal lines that are parallel to the plane remain parallel, but spaced horizontal lines will appear to move closer together as they recede.

When any figure or object is drawn on the picture plane in a way to suggest that it has been seen from one particular viewpoint, it is usually referred to as being drawn in one-point perspective. Similarly, two and three-point perspective refers to figures or objects seen from two or three points of view. The spectator is always considered to be placed at a finite point in relation to the scene or objects and this point can be outside the picture plane.

Drawing systems are not always associated with the illusion of space. Egyptian artists of the period about 2600 BC used a stylised system of representing the visual world on the walls of their tombs. There is no attempt at perspective in these paintings. The relationships of size of the people, animals and objects are governed by their importance for the society for which they were painted. Similarly medieval paintings use a non-illusory system of drawing where symbolism has an important part to play. The needlework record of the Battle of Hastings in 1066, known as the 'Bayeux Tapestry', uses realistic imagery without perspective. In the twentieth century the Cubist paintings of Picasso and Braque also achieve an illusion of space without the use of formal perspective.

Plan

A horizontal section drawn, usually to scale, at a given level (see Fig. 1.2)

Elevation

A vertical section, usually drawn to scale, at a given level (see Fig. 1.3).

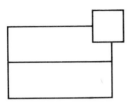

Fig. 1.2   Plan

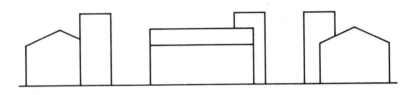

Fig. 1.3   Elevation

Parallel projection

An alternative drawing system to perspective which, while dealing with spatial relationships in a systematic way, does not attempt to give the illusion of depth that is possible with perspective. With parallel projection the spectator is considered to be at infinity and the figures or objects are drawn without any change of scale in relation to their distance from the spectator (see Fig. 1.4). This system cannot, therefore, be used to create images that are intended to represent the illusion of space that can be achieved with perspective.

Orthographic projection

Parallel projections where the projected lines are perpendicular to the picture plane.

Axonometric projection

Orthographic projections in which the figures or objects are inclined in relation to the picture plane. There are three types – isometric, diametric and trimetric – of which the most commonly used are isometric projections, in which all three axes of a rectilinear object are shown at equal angles of 120° to each other, the dimensions along the axes being to the same scale (See Fig. 1.4).

Oblique projection

A parallel projection drawn with one aspect of the scene or object parallel to the picture plane and all other aspects inclined to the plane.

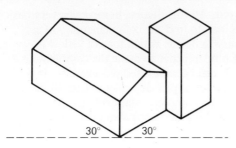

30° 30°

Fig. 1.4   Isometric and Parallel projection

1.4 COLOUR

It is very difficult to be objective about colour, as everyone has a
personal colour vision which is unique.

Colour depends on light. As light varies so colours can appear to
change. What actually changes is our perception of the colour. The
degree of emphasis placed on a range of tones is known as the tonal
value and can help to define colours in a spatial context. Some colours
appear visually to advance while others recede. A useful way of
exploring tonal values is to work in monochrome, a range of tones from
a single colour.

Colours are sometimes divided into warm or cold colours and can
also take on an emotional context. 'Colour harmony' is a term used to
describe a group of colours that appear to work well together. The best
way to gain a knowledge of colour is to experience working from
observation and recording the effects of colour.

Colours can be identified as either *primary* or *secondary*. Primary
colours are red, yellow and blue. These three colours, together with
black and white, are basic to all colour work. Secondary colours are
made by mixing two primary colours together to produce a third
colour:

> red mixed with yellow makes orange;
> yellow mixed with blue makes green;
> blue mixed with red makes violet.

Complementary colours

The primary colours (red, yellow and blue) each have a *complementary*
colour. In theory the way to find the complementary colour of any
primary colour is by mixing together the other two primary colours.
The complementary colour of red, for example, is theoretically made by
mixing yellow and blue together to make green. Green is the

complementary colour of red. All this theory, however, is very basic but confusing. Having decided to find the complementary of a particular red, it is necessary to decide which tone of yellow is needed to mix with which tone of blue in order to make the complementary colour to the original red. It can become a tedious exercise. It is better to design a colour wheel using a set of primary colours with black and white and to make approximate complementary colours as shown in Fig. 1.5. This will involve making decisions about mixing colours.

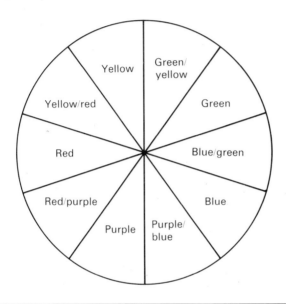

Fig. 1.5   Colour wheel

Another useful experiment is to observe the effects colours have on each other when placed in close proximity. The painter Johannus Itten has done some very interesting research on this (see bibliography (section 4.35) Birren, F. (ed) 1970).

The scientific study of colour and colour systems such as those of Chevreul, Ostwald and Munsell are of specialist interest for the beginner. The study of colour as a branch of physics should not be confused with the study of the appearance of colour.

Colour groups

Yellows:	Naples	Mars
	Lemon	Indian
	Cadmium	Yellow ochre
	Aureolin	Chrome

Reds:	Cadmium	Venetian
	Scarlet	Mars
	Alizarin	Indian
	Carmine	Rose madder
	Crimson Lake	Vermilion
Blues:	Prussian	Phthalocyanine (Phthalo)
	Indigo	Monestial
	Coeruleum	Cobalt
	Permanent	French ultramarine
Greens:	Cadmium	Phthalocyanine (Phthalo)
	Alizarin	Sap
	Monestial	Hookers
	Terre verte	Chrome
	Oxide of chromium	Emerald
	Viridian	Cobalt
	Olive	
Whites:	Flake	Titanium
	Zinc	Chrome
Blacks:	Ivory	Mars
	Lamp	
Browns:	Raw sienna	Burnt sienna
	Raw umber	Burnt umber
	Vandyke brown	

1.5 PAINTING

The development of painting in the twentieth century has brought about radical changes which have also been affected by the availability of new materials.

Traditional oil painting, developed since the sixteenth century, has in many instances given way to work in a variety of different media or combinations of media (mixed media). One of the most significant changes has been the introduction of polymer emulsions. These have enabled painters to increase the scale and speed of their work and break with many of the traditional oil-painting techniques. The new paints can be sprayed, stained, dripped or thrown at the canvas. They can be applied with rollers or decorators' brushes. American painters in the 1940s and 1950s made basic discoveries with these new materials which continue to influence comtemporary painting.

The economics of painting, particularly the high cost of making oil colours from the finest materials, has also increased the widespread substitution of polymer paints for oil colours.

1.6 PAINT/MEDIUMS/BRUSHES/VARNISHES

Acrylic	Aerosol
Alkyd	Egg tempera
Gouache	Metallic
Oil	Pigments
Polymer	Poster
Powder	Water-colour

Acrylic

Paint made using as a binder/medium a man-made resin derived from polymers or copolymers of acrylic acid.

Acrylic paint is fast drying with excellent adhesive qualities. It produces a clear, tough, flexible film that does not crack. The paint will dissolve in water when wet, is easily diluted and is waterproof when dry. By diluting one-to-one with equal parts of water and binder/medium it can be used as water-colour.

Mediums

Acrylic mediums act as a powerful gum as well as a binder. They enable the colour to adhere easily to a variety of surfaces and also help other materials to be incorporated into the paint. Mediums are available in a variety of forms. The most common are liquid, jelly and paste mediums. A gloss medium useful for making glazes of thin, smooth paint and a gel medium for thickening the paint are also available.

Surfaces

Highly absorbent surfaces such as hardboard should be primed with a suitable primer. Some good-quality emulsion paints can be used as primers. A white primed surface will add to the luminosity of the paint. Acrylic paint should not be used on any surface that has been prepared for use with oil paint. Most manufacturers of canvases and boards make special ranges for use with acrylic paint. The cheapest method is to buy unprimed canvas, a suitable set of canvas stretchers and make up the canvas to individual requirements. Robersons have an excellent stock of interchangeable-sized stretchers capable of being made up into a number of finished canvas sizes and they also stock canvas in a choice of grades.

Acrylic varnish

To obtain a gloss finish use a water-based, flexible, transparent, lightfast varnish. This should be applied to the painting about twenty-four hours after it has dried. To stain, spray or apply a wash over a large area use a 'tension breaker' as the medium.

Additives; retarders

To slow down the drying of a painting use a retarder mixed with the colour.

Solvents

For removing areas of dried paint or cleaning colour from brushes or fabrics use an acrylic paint remover or solvent. Avoid using it in a confined space as the fumes could cause distress.

Brushes

No special brushes are required for acrylic paint. Nylon brushes are made for use with this paint but hog hair is quite suitable. Avoid letting the paint dry on the brushes: it is very difficult to remove. Always keep brushes in clean water when not in actual use and wash them thoroughly in soap and warm water when the work is finished. Use only stainless steel knives and a glass, china or plastic palette. Never use a wood palette. Acrylic paint can be used with a roller in the same way as domestic emulsion paint. Clean the roller and paint tray thoroughly after use.

Choice of colours

Winsor & Newton's introductory set of eight colours is a good start for the beginner:

Burnt sienna	Crimson lake
French ultramarine	Mars black
Titanium white	Windsor green
Windsor yellow	Yellow ochre

Also recommended is the Aquatic range made by the American company, Bocour, and sold in the UK by the Acrylic Paint Company. They offer a choice of forty-two colours including iridescents, available in tubes and jars, and a range of mediums suitable for all work in acrylic.

Aerosol

For spray painting to give a waterproof, smooth, matt finish the Marabu Buntlack range of twenty-eight quick-drying colours is ideal. These colours can be used on most surfaces and are made in two sizes, 300 ml and 600 ml. This firm also makes a smaller range of metallic paints in aerosol sprays.

Alkyd colours

A convenient substitute for oil paint, alkyd colours have the advantage of drying quickly. The paint remains workable for the length of a normal working day but will dry overnight. The colours can be reworked after drying by using a special solvent. Alkyd colours mix more easily than acrylic paint. They dry to a hard, elastic, waterproof film which does not crack. They can be thinned with white spirit, turpentine or a proprietary thinner. In this form they can also be applied as a glaze.

Mediums
No special medium is required for alkyd paint. Winsor & Newtons Liquin will increase the translucency and gloss of the paint. For thickening the colours use either Win-Gel or Oleopasto. All these mediums will also improve the drying time. Paste mediums should not be mixed with a brush.

Surfaces
All surfaces suitable for oil painting can be used for alkyd paint. It is possible to mix alkyd and oil paint in the same painting, but always use the slow-drying oil colours on top of the faster-drying alkyd colours.

Varnishes
Use the varnishes available for oil paint. Retouching varnish can be used twenty-four hours after completion. Gloss- and matt-finish varnishes are available and should be added about one month after completion.

Solvents
Winsor & Newton's Winsol is a very strong solvent useful for removing dry alkyd paint. White spirit, petroleum distillate and turpentine will thin colours and will clean wet colour from brushes and palettes.

Brushes
Any brush suitable for use in oil painting can be used for alkyd paint. Always clean off brushes in solvent while working and thoroughly clean them in soap and warm water when finished.

Choice of colours
An introductory set of twelve colours is available. The minimum number of colours for effective working in alkyd is about seven. A beginner could start with tubes of the following colours:

Burnt sienna	Burnt umber
Lemon yellow	Cadmium red
Alizarin crimson	Phthalo blue
Flake white (large tube)	

Egg tempera

Eggs are traditionally used in the kitchen as a binder in cooking recipes and they have a similar binding effect when mixed with powdered pigment. Tempera is one of the oldest methods of easel painting and until the sixteenth century it was the most usual method. The use of egg yolks combined with powdered pigment and water enables the resulting 'tempered' mixture to dry quickly and produce a tough, permanent surface.

Tempera was traditionally used over a gesso ground. This is made from recipes using chalk combined with size and oils and produces a brilliant white painting surface.

Egg tempera can easily be made but must be used very fresh. It is also available ready prepared and makes an excellent underpainting for oil colours. Rowneys make a range of twenty-five colours plus three whites. The book *Materials of the Artist* by Max Doerner (Harrap 1969) gives recipes for making egg tempera and gesso grounds.

Gouache

Gouache is basically opaque water-colour paint. The paint gives a flat, matt finish and is ideal for design work. Gouache is water-soluble and the colours have varying degrees of permanence. They are available in tubes of various sizes. Manufacturers often describe this paint as designers' gouache. It is possible to mix gouache with an acrylic medium which will make the colours waterproof and more easily allow overpainting. The colours can also be sprayed or used with a ruling pen. Gouache is normally intermixable with the whole range of water-soluble paints.

Winsor & Newton make a range of seventy-eight colours and a similar range from Rowney lists sixty colours. Six basic colours, lemon yellow, cadmium red, cobalt blue, viridian green, lampblack and white, will make a useful introduction to this medium.

Metallic paint

One of the most useful ranges of metallic paint is that provided for the car industry. Retouching paint is available in a good range of colours and can be applied by aerosol to most surfaces. The aerosol can must be shaken thoroughly to mix the contents before use. Metallic markers are available from Edding in gold, silver and copper permanent, opaque ink. Rowney make a metallic finish rub-on paste in five finishes.

Oil colours

Oil painting is one of the longest established methods of producing easel pictures. The oil technique probably developed from the tempera methods which flourished up to the sixteenth century, but during the fifteenth century the established form of tempera painting began to be modified by the addition of transparent oil glazes over tempera underpainting. An intermediate stage then followed combining both tempera and oil techniques and this continued until the early seventeenth century.

One of the advantages of oil painting is the slow-drying properties of the oil which allow the painting to be developed layer upon layer with subtle effect. Originally, oil paintings were built up in a long series of carefully planned stages developing from full-scale drawings (sometimes called cartoons) through monochrome underpainting to the final work. Special techniques were developed to modify the later stages by the addition of layers of transparent paint called glazes. Sometimes paint areas were built up by a method known as *scumbling*, using opaque colours partially to overlay each other, giving an uneven effect to parts of the surface of the painting. These traditional methods are still in use and involve building up the painting in a series of layers, with each successive layer containing more medium, known as the fat-over-lean method. Each layer must dry thoroughly before the next is applied. The development of painting in the twentieth century has, however, encouraged the use of alternatives to the oil colour method (see sections on acrylic, alkyd and polymer colours).

It is not necessary for beginners to buy an expensive set of oil colours in a box, or special palettes, knives and easels, or the range of additives which are stocked by art shops. A basic set of colours from one of the inexpensive ranges such as Winsor & Newton's Winton range or Rowney's Georgian range might include the following colours:

Burnt sienna;	Burnt umber;
Lemon yellow;	Cadmium red;
Alizarin crimson;	Prussian blue;
Flake white (large tube)	

Add to this a bottle of good-quality linseed oil from a hardware shop, white spirit for thinning, a metal plate for use as a palette, some inexpensive hog-hair brushes, old rags and a suitably primed sheet of hardboard and this should complete a basic kit.

It is possible to make oil colours by mixing finely ground pigments with a good-quality linseed oil and petroleum distillate. There are also several types of medium on the market which can be added directly to ground pigment for making oil colours (see also section on pigments).

It is advisable to avoid purchasing tins of paint which dry out quickly once opened. Tubes of paint come in various sizes: the 22 ml to 38 ml size is practical for most purposes. Flake white should be purchased in the largest size available as it is likely that more of this colour will be used than any other.

Mediums

Oil colours are soluble in turpentine or white spirit when wet. The usual medium is linseed oil, but poppy oil or safflower oil are also suitable. Another alternative is an alkyd medium, which has a shorter drying time than oil.

Surfaces

Canvas is the traditional surface for oil painting. It is manufactured both primed and unprimed. The cheapest is unprimed cotton. Other materials used are flax and jute. Canvas can be bought in widths up to 2.1 m (84 in) wide, but wider canvas can be purchased on special order.

Stretchers

Canvas must be stretched, ready for priming and painting, on special stretchers. It is possible to buy canvas ready-stretched, but it is much cheaper to purchase interchangeable stretcher pieces and buy canvas by the yard or metre. A variety of interlockable stretcher pieces will enable a number of canvas sizes to be made up. For stretching canvas a pair of special pliers is very useful.

Hardboard is recommended as an alternative to the more expensive stretched canvas. It is stable and can be reused if thoroughly rubbed down. A good-quality grade should be purchased and the painting carried out on the smooth side. The textured side produces a mechanical pattern in the surface of the hardboard which is difficult to eradicate. Large sheets of hardboard need strengthening at the back to prevent warping. All surfaces need careful priming to avoid the colour being absorbed into the surface. A good-quality emulsion paint is suitable. Several coats may be necessary to obtain a good luminous painting surface.

Brushes

It is worth investing in good-quality brushes. Always buy the best brushes that can be afforded. Cheap brushes soon lose their hairs and shape. For fine, detailed work sable brushes are ideal. They are very expensive, however, and blended hair brushes are a good alternative for the beginner. Hog hair is the traditional oil colour brush. Aluminium or seamless nickel-plated ferrules are preferable to tin ferrules as they will not rust. Always dry brushes thoroughly after cleaning and leave them upright when not in use.

Oil brushes are made in a range of eighteen sizes from the smallest, 1, to the largest size, 18. There are eleven types of brush heads of which four types are most commonly used: Pointed (round); Square short (bright); square long; Filbert. A basic set of brushes should include at least one of each of these types. A No. 3 Pointed, No. 6 Square short, No. 8 Square long, a No. 10 Square long and a Filbert would be useful for the beginner.

Additives/varnishes/drying oils/mediums
Oils added to oil colours vary the drying rate of the colour. There are two main types of oils:
1. Linseed oils: Stand oil (pale) and refined/purified oils will slow the drying time.
2. Drying oils such as poppy/safflower oils will speed the drying time.
The addition of oil to the colours will affect their consistency.

Solvents
Solvents will dilute the oil colours. There are four main types:
1. Turpentine. This liquid will thicken if constantly exposed to light.
2. White spirit. Cheap – available in litre cans from DIY shops.
3. Petroleum distillate. This will slow the drying rate of oil colours when used as a medium.
4. Oil of lavender. Dries slowly.
    It is cheaper to buy solvents from hardware or DIY shops, but the quality will not be as good as the types specially prepared for painters. It is also possible, but unnecessary, to buy ready-prepared mediums which are a mixture of oil and solvent.

Varnishes
Varnish has two main uses:
1. To restore the colour where a dull effect has been produced:
2. To give an all-over protective film to the finished painting.
    Varnish tends to affect the character of the original colours although it will not darken oil colour. It is not usual to varnish a painting which has a heavy impasto effect unless it is necessary to use the varnish as a binder to hold the paint together. Varnish should always be used in moderation and preferably not at all. The main types of varnish are:
1. *Picture varnish*: Available in aerosols for coating the whole surface of a painting. It gives a slight gloss to the picture surface.
2. *Matt varnish*: Similar to picture varnish but giving a matt effect.
3. *Copal varnish*: Can be used as a medium for enhancing colours or, when diluted with white spirit, as a permanent varnish.
4. *Damar varnish*: Useful for restoring flat colours on an otherwise gloss or semi-gloss painting surface.
5. *Mastic varnish*: A removable varnish.

Pigments

A solid substance, organic or inorganic, which when finely ground is used to give colour to paint or varnish. Ground pigments are mixed with a binder to hold the pigment together. These binders are also sometimes known as mediums. The type of binder/medium depends on the type of paint to be produced.

Manufacturers add to the bound pigment additives such as driers to increase the rate at which the paint dries, or retarders to slow the drying rate. All paint-makers have their own formulas for making paint and these are continually being improved. This sometimes means that paint from more than one manufacturing source is not intermixable.

Polymer paints

There are two main types of polymer synthetic resin used in paint manufacture:
1. Polyvinyl acetate (PVA);
2. Acrylic (polymer or co-polymers).

Resins are combined with pigment and additives to produce paint which is available in tubes and other containers. Polymer paint can easily be made by adding a suitable polymer binder to powdered pigment. The only other medium required is water.

Suitable polymer binders are Rowney PVA Medium; Cryla Gloss; Matt and Glaze Mediums; Berol's Marvin PVA; and Winsor & Newton's Nacryl Acrylic Medium. Pigments available include Rowney's finely-ground pigments supplied in 1 oz bottles or 1 lb jars. Thirty-eight pigments are available. Winsor & Newton list sixty-one dry ground pigments available in 60 ml glass pots or 500 g packs.

Polymer paints are fast drying and have resistance to yellowing. They will not crack and their excellent adhesive qualities enable them to be used on a variety of surfaces. The colours are intermixable within the individual manufacturer's colour ranges. They dissolve in water when wet, are easily diluted and are waterproof when dry. The paint can be used as a glaze, for impasto work and for spraying. It can be applied in a variety of ways including by brush, knife and roller. Polymer paints dry quickly, so it is important to keep all implements in water when not in use. Cleaning should be in warm water with soap. A china, glass or plastic palette is ideal and can be cleaned with water if the paint is moist or scraped with a knife if it is dry. Always replace the tops of tubes and other containers immediately after use and ensure that the inside and rims of tops are clean. The medium acts as a strong adhesive and it is difficult to remove the tops from jars which have been left dirty. A small amount of water added to the top of paint containers before sealing will prevent paint from drying out.

Choice of colours

Rowney Cryla and Flow formulas are available in thirty-eight colours. Their Redicolor range has sixteen colours and their PVA range twenty colours. Winsor & Newton Acrylic colours are available in thirty colours and their Vinyl colour has a choice of twenty-one colours. This firm's Vinyl colours are also available in 1 litre plastic buckets. The introductory set of eight colours from Winsor & Newton is suitable for the beginner (see also acrylic, p. 22)

Poster colours

Poster colour is a form of gouache which is opaque, water-soluble and ready for use from either tubes or the more familiar small glass pots. Poster colours are cheaper than designers' gouache. If funds are limited they are a useful alternative and they can be mixed with a number of other water-soluble paints. They are available in a large range of colours, but a set of six should be enough for a start: Lemon yellow; Otswald blue; Otswald red; Scarlet; Prussian blue or black; White.

A metal or china plate as a palette and a jam jar is a useful water container.

Brushes

Soft brushes are essential. Do not use hog hair. Choose water-colour brushes from the most expensive range if possible. The price of brushes varies according to the type of hair used in the brush, from the very expensive sable to brushes made of a selection of mixed hairs from several sources.

A set of five brushes should be sufficient. Try numbers 0, 3, 5, 7 and 12. Aluminium or nickel-plated ferrules are best because they will not rust. Always repoint brushes when cleaned and store them upright.

Powder paint

The easiest form of paint mixing is powder colour and water. The result is a form of gouache or poster colour, very opaque and effective for bold design work. When mixed with a polymer medium such as one of the PVA mediums, the qualities of powder colour are greatly enhanced. The adhesive quality of the PVA enables the resulting paint to be used with effect on all types of surfaces. Large-scale, inexpensive, mural projects are therefore possible. The paint can be applied with rollers or ordinary household paint-brushes or the more refined water-colour brushes. Remember to wash out all brushes and other equipment thoroughly immediately after use. Powder paint is available in a limited range of colours.

Water-colour

Ground pigments mixed with water-soluble gums. This type of painting was developed in England in the late eighteenth and early nineteenth centuries. The water-soluble, translucent colours rely for their distinctive effect on the whiteness of the paper being overlaid with washes of transparent colour, with the thinnest colours being applied first. Pure water-colour painting is still a highly regarded craft, but many painters and illustrators now combine water-colour with other water-soluble media.

Water-colours are obtainable in the traditional box with replaceable pans or in tubes. The scale of water-colour painting is limited so the colours usually last for quite a long time. When purchasing tubes the smallest size may therefore be the best. The colours can be applied with brushes, sponges, soft cloths or fingers. If brushes are needed remember that water-colour painting can be done with any brush suitable for water-soluble paint. Find a personal method of working. There are lots of theories about how to paint in water-colours, but one of the greatest water-colour painters, J. M. W. Turner (1775–1851), experimented with these colours to great effect and did not conform to any rules.

The choice of paper is very important. It has to take heavy amounts of water and special care must be taken in choosing a good-quality paper. One way of effectively using a cheap paper is first to dampen it thoroughly with cold water, then fix it to the surface of a drawing-board by using gummed tape around the edges. Allow the paper to dry thoroughly before starting work and, on completion, cut the finished painting free from the board.

Some colours fade when constantly exposed to direct sunlight and care should be taken to protect finished work.

Water-colours are made in several grades. For beginners the cheapest grade is quite satisfactory. A set of six colours should be enough to allow for some experimentation: Lemon yellow; Vermilion; Crimson alizarin; Cobalt blue; Indigo; Viridian; Water-colour brushes are available in sixteen sizes from the smallest size 000 to the largest size 14. Numbers 1, 3, 5, 7 and 10 will give a good range of brush marks. Take great care of brushes. Wash thoroughly after use, repoint carefully with the fingers and store with the brush hairs upwards. The price range of watercolour brushes is very wide and the larger sizes in the best-quality series are very expensive. Fortunately, manufacturers also make much cheaper brushes and, for beginners, the Series 32 blended-hair brushes with seamless aluminium ferrules from Winsor & Newton are good value.

1.7 BOARDS/PAPERS/SKETCH-BLOCKS/PADS

Boards

The word 'board' is used to describe a range of backings lined or surfaced with paper. Boards are made in a variety of thicknesses or weights and (see p. 33) and the papers are fixed to the surface of the board using special glues. Some boards have paper surfaces on both sides. The thicker the board the more stable will be the working surface. There are three main types of board which are in common use:

1. Bristol Board. A pasteboard with a smooth surface ideal for preparing work for reproduction. It is available, in a range of thicknesses up to four-sheet (see p. 33) and a choice of sizes, from several suppliers including Daler, Rowney and Winsor & Newton. Frisk stock a double-sided board particularly suitable for work in technical and fashion illustration.
2. Line board. The most famous line board is CS10 which is hand finished and will stand erasion. Line boards are used for all types of line drawing and illustration. They will normally take work in line, wash and airbrush.
3. Mounting and display boards. There is a very wide range of lined boards available for finished work. Berol, Daler and Rowney all have good ranges, and for more specialist use Oram and Robertson have a good choice of white-lined boards in a variety of thicknesses. Frisk have five different types of board including a double-sided lined board in black and white, a dry mounting white-lined board and a display board 1524 × 1016 mm (60 × 40) in which is white-lined on both sides. They also stock a board which has a different colour shade on each side. Coloured boards are also available from several other manufacturers. One of the largest ranges is from Daler who have a choice of fifty-eight colours in their Studland and Ingres ranges. The Colourmount boards from Slater Harrison have a range of twenty-seven colours in both four- and six-sheet thicknesses. This firm's Inglevale range has a choice of five sheet sizes from 508 × 635 mm (20 in × 25 in) up to 1524 × 1016 mm (60 in × 40 in) in a wide range of thicknesses. These boards have a smooth, white, opaque surface on both sides.

Papers

Choosing the correct or most suitable paper is important if the best results are to be obtained. Papers in common use are:

Art	Card
Cartridge	Conservation/Repairing
Cover	Crepe
Drawing	Fluorescent
Gummed	Handmade
Ingres	Kraft
Metal foil	Newsprint
Poster (MG)	Poster
Print-making	Sugar
Specialist	Translucent
Tissue	
Water-colour	

Traditionally, papers used by artists and designers were made by hand from rags, but in nearly all cases this process has been replaced by machine or mould-made methods using a variety of materials including wood pulp and cotton. It is still possible to obtain handmade papers which are easily identified by their naturally irregular edges.

The best machine-made papers have a high cellulose content and are made from cotton, straw, esparto grass, sawdust, bamboo, hemp, jute and wood. Inexpensive papers tend to be made from esparto grass and wood mixtures. The strongest papers are made from materials with the longest fibres. Paper processing affects the nature of the finished paper. The strength of a machine-made paper tends to follow the grain. Handmade papers, having no obvious grain, have an even strength over the whole surface. Japanese papers, obtainable from several manufacturers including T. N. Lawrence & Son, are replacing some traditional European handmade papers. They are usually unsized that is untreated with size and therefore need careful handling and are often made from fibres derived from the mulberry, used in Japan for the feeding of silkworms for the production of silk.

Plastic papers are becoming more readily available. The surfaces vary from glossy to semi-matt and matt and these papers can be very strong and washable.

Paper quantities are usually measured in quires of 25 sheets or reams of 500 sheets.

Papers, and the boards on which they are supported, are sold in a variety of sizes, weights and quantities. Although standards of the International Standards Organisation (ISO) are being applied to the paper industry, it is still possible to find other metric and imperial sizes quoted.

The main methods of determining the amount of paper to be purchased is by specifying the sheet size, weight and quantity. The density of the paper has an effect on the weight and this can be deceptive when comparing the weight of one paper against another.

The thickness of lined boards is usually represented by reference to the calliper measurement expressed in 1,000ths of an inch, i.e. calliper 0.030 in. The gradual conversion to metric systems means that boards can also be shown in micron thicknesses: 1 micron = 1000th of a centimetre, i.e. 1,250 microns = 1.25 mm thick.

The weight of papers and boards is now almost universally given as grams per square metre (gsm or g/m^2). When imperial weights are used the references are to the weight per ream, i.e. 45 lb, 60 lb, or 140 lb.

Papers and boards are made with a variety of surfaces. The most common are:

(a) Hot Press (HP)   a smooth surface;
(b) NOT   a slightly rough surface;
(c) Rough.

In the following descriptions of papers, where a paper is also available as a lining on a board, the letter (B) is shown after the name or type of the paper.

Art paper

This is traditionally a china-clay coated paper which is mechanically passed through rollers to produce a hard, smooth surface. The term 'art paper' is used in a more general way and it is important to be specific if traditional art paper is required.

Card

A stiff paper useful for work where a flexible material is required. Card is very adaptable and can be rolled, twisted and easily cut. It is capable of taking thin washes of colour and can be used with a wide range of drawing media. Card has specific uses in fashion design, model-making, stage design and three-dimensional work of all kinds. It is also extensively used for display purposes.

Cartridge paper

This is the most common of all papers used for general drawing and is widely available in a variety of sheet and roll sizes and weights. The paper has a closely woven texture.

Conservation papers

Barcham Green make special handmade papers for conservation work. They offer four types of papers, all available with NOT surface. The Bodleian Light Toned Laid is made in two weights, 22 lb and 32 lb in Super Royal size (19 × 27 in). The Dover Dark Toned Laid is made in Medium size 17½ × 23¼ in at 20 lb weight. India Office is the name of a paper, brown wove, available in Imperial size (22 × 30 in) at 90 lb weight. This firm also supply machine-made, light-weight, long-fibred tissues for repairing archival material by lamination. They are known as L2, M and Eltoline. A special heavy, wet-strength, absorbent paper developed for the Public Records Office and known as Multisorb can be used for pressing documents. Barcham Green will also make special papers to customers' individual requirements.

Cover paper

Originally produced to form the outside covers of books, this paper is now used for a wide range of purposes including work in chalk and pastel. The paper has a matt surface and can be obtained in a wide range of sheet sizes and weights. Daler have one of the largest colour ranges of forty colours.

Crêpe Paper

This paper has an elastic quality with a colour range which is ideal for display work. The colours are, however, quickly affected by exposure to sunlight and rapid fading can occur. Crêpe paper is not suitable for use with paint.

Drawing paper

This is the generic name given to a large range of papers including those sometimes classified as cartridge papers. Some papers in this group have the trade names of the makers such as Hollingworth Drawing Papers, which are ideal for architectural and engineering drawing and for designers' pencil roughs. Drawing papers are usually available with a choice of surfaces.

Fluorescent papers (B)
A range of very brightly coloured papers suitable for display purposes. Berol and Daler both have good colour ranges. The Day-Glo range from Slater Harrison includes plain, gummed, pulp and ticket boards in six colours.

Gummed papers
Available with either a smooth, shiny or matt surface with a gummed back in a wide range of colours. The paper is sold in squares, sheets or rolls and is ideal for decorative work.

Handmade papers
Traditional handmade papers are now difficult to obtain as only a few manufacturers still produce sufficient quantities for commercial production. The firm of Barcham Green make an excellent range of papers for a variety of purposes.

Ingres papers
These papers have a soft, textured, fibrous surface. A particularly good-quality paper is the Swedish Tumba containing 50 per cent rag. Daler have one of the largest colour ranges with seventeen colours. The paper is particularly suitable for work in pastels and charcoal.

Kraft paper
A strong brown paper particularly useful for pen, ink and wash drawing. Available in sheets and rolls from several firms including Oram and Robertson.

Metal foil papers
Available in gold, silver and a range of colours in sheets or rolls. Reeves stock three colours, red, green and blue. Very useful for decorative and display work.

Newsprint
An absorbent, unsized paper sometimes known as kitchen paper. Newsprint is similar to papers used for the production of newspapers. It is cheap but thin. Available in sheets and rolls and particularly useful for proof printing of all kinds.

Poster paper (MG)
An uncoated paper, machine-glazed (MG) and polished to give a high gloss on one side. These papers are primarily for use as posters and the

sizes available correspond to the sizes of poster sites. Ideal for screen printing. (see p. 46).

Poster paper (B)

Papers designed for display purposes are also known as poster papers. The Ingersley range from Slater Harrison is available in sixteen colours in both sheet and roll. This firm also has a seven-colour range of poster lined boards.

Print making papers

Barcham Green's handmade print-making papers are available in student packages of second-quality papers containing 25 kg of paper, approximately between 200 and 400 sheets. This firm make three papers for use by print-makers. The Crisbrook is a white etching and lithographic paper, soft and unsized (waterleaf). Made with 100 per cent cotton, it is available in NOT and HP surfaces in Imperial size and Wealden size (approximately $22\frac{1}{2} \times 31$ in). Boughton and Boxley are two neutrally-sized papers suitable for all print-making techniques. Boughton has a warm, white colour and Boxley is pale duck-egg blue, both available in NOT and HP surfaces in Imperial size. India Office and Turner Grey are two well-sized, tinted papers. India Office is a pale brown colour and Turner Grey is a blue/grey with a mix of black fibres. Available in NOT surface only in Imperial size.

Specialist papers

CS2 (B).   A white paper ideal for illustration work using gouache, water-colours or dyes. Available as either HP or NOT surface in sheets and pads.

CS10.   An excellent paper for line work. This paper will take repeated erasings but will also give a clear image when used with a light box. Particularly recommended for technical illustrations. Available in pads and sheets.

Hollingsworth Kent paper (B).   This paper, which is available in HP and NOT surfaces, is recommended for work with designers' colours and gouache. Available from Frisk, Daler with Winsor & Newton.

Line papers (B).   In addition to the CS papers, a number of manufacturers make line papers. The Artline range of lined boards from Slater Harrison includes a smooth quality board suitable for finished artwork. Daler Superline boards are available in Double Imperial, Imperial and Half-Imperial sizes. Daler also make a Pasteline board specially developed for paste-up work. This firm's Superline paper is ideal for fine line work and can be purchased in pads or Imperial-sized sheets.

Sugar paper

A strong, absorbent paper with a toothed surface.* Available in a range of colours from Reeves and Berol. Suitable for work in powder colour, pastel, charcoal and crayon.

Tissue paper

Semi-transparent paper available in an excellent range of colours. The colours fade rapidly in strong sunlight and the paper will not take water or paint. Ideal for collage and all kinds of display work. Berol have a good range of colours.

Translucent papers

These tracing papers are made for specialist activities and have a high degree of transparency, together with an evenness of texture. It is important to protect the papers from variations in temperature or humidity which can affect the surface. Available in a variety of sizes and qualities. For general use the Winsor and Newton and Reeves ranges are ideal. For specialist use the range of papers from Frisk, particularly their pads in A1, A2, A3 and A4 sizes (see Section 4.3) are excellent for design studio use.

Watercolour papers

T. H. Saunders (B). A pure, rag-mould*, water-colour paper available with NOT, rough or HP surfaces and acid free to provide colour stability. Available from several firms including Rowney, Frisk, Winsor & Newton and Daler.

Bockingford. A pure, wood-pulp, mould-made water-colour paper which takes washes particularly well. Acid free. This paper is less expensive than T. H. Saunders. Widely available from several firms including Frisk, Winsor & Newton and Daler.

Barcham Green (B). Royal Watercolour Society handmade water-colour paper available in three surfaces, rough, NOT and HP. This paper is produced to meet the requirements of the Royal Society of Painters in Water-colours.

Water-colour pads

Papers suitable for use with water-colours are also made up into pads, usually of A2, A3, A4 and A5 sizes. Rowney has two qualities of paper, the Artist Water-colour Paper and the inexpensive Georgian Water-colour Paper, made up into pads in this way.

Sketch-blocks

Sketch-blocks and pads are designed with a firm board base on which to work, with the top sheet having to be removed before work can commence on the following sheet. They are generally intended for use as either drawing or water-colour paper. Several manufacturers specialise in producing water-colour papers assembled in blocks and the papers available include T. H. Saunders and Bockingford.

Sketch-books

There are two main types of sketch-books. The more permanent type has sheets of good-quality paper carefully bound within stiff covers. The other type has detachable sheets, usually spiral bound. A sketch-book is an essential item for all artists and designers. It is one of the most useful ways of keeping together, in sequence, visual observations and notes. The famous sketch-books of Leonardo da Vinci are a supreme example of this kind of record. It is worth investing in a good-quality sketch-book with bound sheets rather than a spiral-bound book which is more difficult to maintain. Books containing excellent papers, including Saunders rough and NOT surfaces, are available and sometimes inexpensive books can be bought where a paper supplier or printer has bound together good-quality offcuts. Suppliers of good-quality bound sketch-books include Robersons and Rowney. Spiral-bound sketch-books are generally more easily available than the spine-bound type. The average paper weight is between 70 and 100 gsm and the range of sizes is from A1 to A5. Spiral pads are obtainable from several firms including Daler, Reeves, and Winsor & Newton.

Pads

Studio Pads/Layout pads

These are ideal pads for studio roughs and for the development of ideas in a visual form. Several firms produce high-quality paper pads, including Frisk who have a comprehensive range covering presentation, layout, marker, scrap, detail and tracing pads. All, except the marker and scrap pads, are available in four sheet sizes, A1 to A4. The A plus pads from Schoellershammer are highly recommended. The paper is made from dust bulk and is hand finished. The sheet size, although described using the ISO 'A' sizes, includes a border which allows for marginal sketches, trim lines, registration marks and notes. A similar range of tracing pads is also available. Other normal A-size pads can be obtained from Daler who make an eighty-sheet pad in A2, A3 and A4 sheet sizes.

Tracing pads

Tracing pads are affected by changes in temperature and humidity which can cause cockling of the paper surface. Pads should be shrink-wrapped by the manufacturer. Frisk make two pads, one a lightweight pad (60/65 gsm) and one medium weight (90 gsm). Both pads are shrink-wrapped. Daler make fifty-sheet pads in A2, A3 and A4 sizes, 90 gsm called the 'D' series. For artists they make a 60 gsm paper pad called the 'A' series. The Hammer Microdraft tracing paper from UNO (a division of A-Wick & Partners Ltd) is available in 63, 90 and 112 gsm.A0 to A4 sheets or in 762, 841 and 1,016 mm wide rolls.

1.8 PRINT-MAKING

The making of printed images on various surfaces is a well-established and traditional activity for both fine artists and print-makers. The making of a limited number of prints, known as an edition, is an effective way to control the production and price of prints. The development of photography has also given further encouragement to print-making and, for the popular market, the techniques of offset lithography and screen printing have enabled very large numbers of print reproductions to be cheaply and relatively quickly produced.

Limited editions
This term is used to refer to a small number of prints which are authorised by the artist and usually printed under the artist's control. They provide a guarantee to the purchaser that not more than a stated number of prints will be made and each print is signed and numbered by the artist.

Proof prints
Technically this is a print from the early, proofing stage of production. These prints are often hand-printed by the artist and, because of their rarity, are usually sold at a higher price than a limited edition. Proof prints are always individually signed and numbered by the artist.

Unlimited editions
With this type of print there is no control over the number of prints made and production can often run into thousands of copies. The artist's signature is mechanically reproduced and the prints are not numbered.

Reproductions.   These are not prints but commercial copies, often varying in size from the original.

Original prints by artists such as Rembrandt and Goya are sometimes sold by auction in the major sale-rooms or can be purchased through fine-art★ dealers. A number of galleries specialise in the sale of prints by contemporary artists. Outstanding collections of prints are held by the British Museum Print Room and the Victoria and Albert Museum Print Room, and most provincial and national galleries have important collections. There is a large collection of contemporary prints at the Tate Gallery.

There are three main classes of print-making: relief-printing; intaglio; planographic. Each of these methods is described below.

Relief-printing

Woodcuts

The ideal wood for woodcuts is soft with an even grain. The most commonly used is pear, but lime, cherry and sycamore can also be effective. The size of the 'block' is a matter of individual choice, but if it is intended to use it in conjunction with type its height must be the same as that of the type (2.33 cm). It is essential, too, that its sides be square so that it can be fitted alongside type in the printing 'frame'. Woodcuts should not be confused with wood engravings (described below). A woodcut print uses the flat surface of the wood with the grain running lengthways. It is useful to have a clear idea of the scale of the image to be made before cutting, but as the method of cutting is quite different from that of drawing it is sometimes best to let the image develop as the cutting proceeds rather than have too precise an idea of what to expect. Remember, the printed image on the paper will be the reverse of the image cut on the block. If it is decided to draw direct on to the wood before cutting, then it is helpful to cover the cutting surface with a wash of process white such as that of Winsor & Newton, which is available in 14 ml, 80 ml and 100 ml pots. This will help to define the drawn image more clearly. Images can also be transferred to the block by using tracing paper which, when placed face down on the wood and redrawn from the back, will transfer the image to the block. It is also possible to cover the cutting area with a photographic emulsion, in controlled lighting conditions and thereby transfer images from film negatives.

Woodcutting tools

Any cutting tool will be effective on soft wood. The type of blade and the amount of pressure applied will influence the kind of mark and the subsequent effect on the print. Special woodcutting tools are available, such as gouges and scrives of various dimensions. All tools should be kept very sharp and not allowed to come into contact with anything other than soft wood. Suppliers of wood blocks include T. N. Lawrence, who also stock all the tools necessary for woodcutting.

Printing

Any paint or ink can be used for printing, and experimentation will produce a variety of images from the same block. If it is necessary to obtain an even cover of ink then specially prepared colours and a hand-printing roller should be used. The printing ink should be placed on a sheet of glass, evenly rolled and then lightly applied to the cut surface of the block. The block should then be firmly placed face down on the printing surface. Soft papers will take the image with the minimum amount of pressure. Heavier paper may require the use of a press. Blocks can be used for printing on a wide variety of surfaces including fabrics and plastics. Printing inks suitable for beginners are available from several firms including Rowne, Reeves, Winsor & Newton and T. N. Lawrence. Handmade printing papers are available from Barcham Green. A woodcut by Dürer is shown in Fig. 1.6.

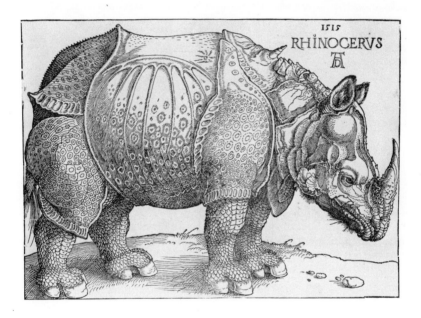

Fig. 1.6 Woodcut – 'A Rhinoceros' by A. Dürer (dated 1515)

Linocuts

Lino is an inexpensive and effective method of relief-printing. It is available from Winsor & Newton in four sizes up to 305 × 254 mm. It is quite thick and has a plain, brown surface. Rowney stock lino in 1.5 × 900 mm rolls and T. N. Lawrence can supply lino mounted on wood to type height. The method of working is similar to that for woodcuts, but a major advantage in using lino is that the cuts can be made in any direction. Special lino-cutting tools can be obtained such as Mitchell's lino cutters, which are made in a variety of shapes and are available in sets. Lino can be mounted on wood, chipboard or blockboard for printing and, if type high, can be printed alongside letterpress type. Large-scale linocuts are possible and all prints can be taken through several stages of develement varying the printing, cutting and colours at each stage. The prints can be made using either oil or water-based inks. Oil-based printing inks are available from Reeves in a limited range of ten colours, plus black and white, and from T. N. Lawrence who stock a range of forty-three colours, together with black and white. White spirit is needed to clean rollers and other utensils after printing with oil-based inks. A linocut by Michael Rothenstein is shown in Fig. 1.7.

Fig. 1.7   Linocut – 'Cockerel Turning Round' (1956) by Michael Rothenstein

Wood engraving

This method of relief-printing enables subtle and sophisticated images to be produced by cutting the close-textured end grain of boxwood. This wood, however, is quite difficult to handle and great care should be taken to prevent it from splitting. T. N. Lawrence stocks suitable end-grain* blocks, type high and made to any size. Engraving can also be done on plastic sheets and nickel-plated metal sheets. Such engravings lack the delicate characteristics of wood engravings, but do provide a more stable working surface. The technique of traditional wood engraving favours the development of small, delicate images and a master of this method of relief-printing was Thomas Bewick (1753–1828). An example of Bewick's work is shown in Fig. 1.8.

Fig. 1.8   Wood-engraving – 'Snipe' by Thomas Bewick from British Water Birds (1825)

Tools

There are two basic tools used for wood engraving. Line-making tools and scaupers for clearing areas of wood. Either type of cutter is set in a wooden handle, which is placed at an angle to the blade, to ensure that the tool can be placed very close to the working surface to give maximum control of the image. It is possible to obtain tools made to individual requirements, but a set of standard tools is quite suitable for the beginner. The line tools are called *gravers* and the tools for cutting curved lines are called *spitstickers*. A large *spitsticker* is called a *bullsticker*. For hatching and producing even tones a tint tool is needed. Always keep tools very sharp and only use them for engraving purposes. T. N. Lawrence can supply a range of suitable tools.

Process

Wood engraving is carried out on a circular, leather pad filled with sand and known, appropriately, as a sandbag. Always work by turning the sandbag for changes in the direction of the cuts and never cut with the tool pointing towards the body.

Intaglio printing

Intaglio printing surfaces have the ink-carrying portions hollowed out; the whole surface is ink-covered then cleaned off, leaving the hollows filled with ink which is transferred when paper is pressed into contact. There are five intaglio printing methods in common use and these may be successfully combined to make mixed-media prints. All the methods use a metal plate as the vehicle for taking the image and transferring it to the paper. The traditional plate is copper, but zinc and steel plates are cheaper and, for etching in colour, steel plates should be used. The plates can be incised (etching, line engraving, drypoint), or the image developed by a combination of incised line and tone, or entirely tonal (mezzotint). The intaglio process is popular with fine artists and print-makers because of the individuality that can be sustained through the various methods, and the way that the image can be changed. Modern commercial printing methods now produce reproductions of intaglio prints which, however, lack the character of the originals.

Etching

Etching is the most popular of the intaglio methods. A coloured acid resist* ground is first spread over the plate. Then a special needle is used to draw through the ground and the marks made by the needle are subsequently bitten out by treatment in a nitric acid bath. The depth of the bite depends on the length of time the plate is left in the acid solution. Acid solution must always be made by adding the acid to water.

After treatment in the acid bath the plate is removed, cleaned and inked with a gauze pad or leather 'dolly'. Surplus ink is cleaned off with gauze and the flat side of the hand. The ink has now been forced into the areas burnt by the acid and the image originally drawn by the needle is then ready for printing.

The scale of etchings can vary from quite small areas about the size of postage stamps to large, poster-size prints. The process involves the use of dangerous acids and great care must be taken not to inhale the fumes and to wear protective gloves and clothing. Special exhibitions of etchings are occasionally mounted by such institutions as the British Museum, which has an outstanding collection, and the Victoria and Albert Museum.

An alternative method to the needle-drawn etching is photo-etching (see Fig. 1.9). With this method photographic images can be transferred to a photo-sensitised plate, prepared in controlled lighting conditions.

Materials for etching can usually be obtained from T. N. Lawrence, Robersons and L. Cornellissen.

Line engraving

This is a direct drawing method on to a plate using a line tool called a Burin. It produces the most delicate drawn lines which are ideal for small-scale work. The plate is subsequently inked as for etching and printed on paper under pressure.

Drypoint

A similar method to line engraving. Drypoint uses a special steel point to scratch a line on to a plate. This method allows for freedom in the

Fig. 1.9 Photo-etching – General Dynamics FUN 1965–70 'Transparent Creatures Hunting New Victims' by Eduardo Paolozzi

style of drawing and can be effectively combined with line engraving. The image has a short life, however, and few identical impressions can be taken. The inking process is the same as for etching.

Aquatint

This method enables tonal areas to be produced and can be combined with line techniques. Areas of tone are achieved by dusting the surface of the plate with granulated resin which is then melted over a low flame such as a Bunsen burner. This results in a grainy, porous surface through which nitric acid solution can bite, producing areas of tone to replace the areas dusted with the resin. These areas will, of course, be dark areas on the final print. To produce white areas it is necessary to stop out or isolate parts of the plate with a special varnish before dusting the surface with resin. An example of an aquatint is shown in Fig. 1.10.

Mezzotint

This process produces prints which are entirely tonal. The surface of the plate is abraded and tonal areas of great subtlety can be achieved by reducing, stage by stage, the depth of the abrasion. White areas are burnished and left smooth. This method can also be used in combination with other intaglio methods.

Printing papers

Unsized papers are ideal for intaglio as they are more absorbent and flexible. All the processes use dampened paper placed under pressure for printing. For information on suitable papers see the section on print-making papers, page 36.

Planographic printing

Planographic printing surfaces are level and prepared so that ink is accepted by some parts of the surface and not by the other parts. Ink-accepting parts of the surface may be greasy, the other parts being moist and ink-rejecting.

Screen printing

This is a method of printing images on a variety of surfaces, both two and three-dimensional, by forcing ink through a stencilled screen of fabric or metal mesh rather like forcing flour through a sieve. This method is particularly suitable for printing flat areas of colour and is capable of using both drawn and photographic images.

Two-dimensional screen printing on paper or fabric is the most commonly used system and is, therefore, the method dealt with in this section. The basic equipment needed is a wooden frame to carry the stretched screen; a suitable screen material such as organdie, silk, nylon or Terylene; a rubber squeegee for forcing the ink through the stretched screen and a drying rack to allow the printed surfaces to dry without touching one another.

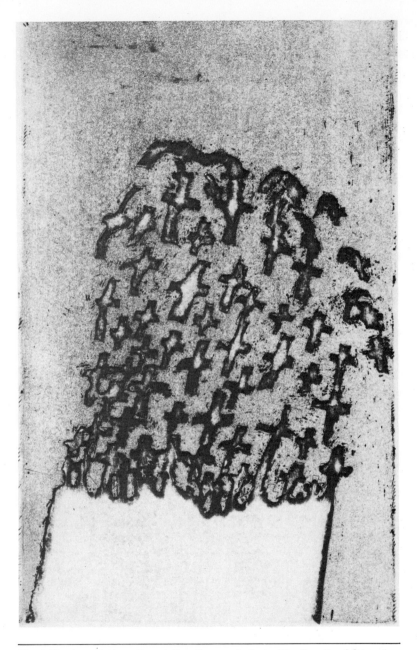

Fig. 1.10   Aquatint by a Foundation Course student of the Faculty of Art and
Design – Barnet College

The wooden frame. The size of the frame determines the printing area but, as it is always possible to utilise a large frame for the simultaneous printing of more than one separate image, the smallest practical size needed is about 0.6 × 1 m (2 × 3 ft) inside-frame measurement. A separate frame is, ideally, needed for each colour to be printed, so work in four colours could require four frames. Frames can be handmade or purchased ready-made from a specialist supplier such as Sericol. In order to ensure that the colours are printed in exactly the same place on each print (correctly registered) the screen frame should be fixed to the base of the printing table and the corners of the sheets of paper marked on the table.

Screen fabrics One of the best fabrics for making the screen is silk, hence the term silk-screen printing. The mesh of screen fabrics is graded from fine to coarse in a range of about fifty grades. Coarse grades have about 18 meshes to the square inch (size 0000) and the finest grades have about 200 meshes to the square inch (size 25). The coarser the mesh the heavier will be the deposit of ink on the printed surface. The fabric should be stretched on the frame using staples fired from a staple gun. It is important to obtain an evenly tensioned screen. Screen fabrics may need degreasing before use and suitable degreasers are available from Pronk, Davis and Rusby and Sericol.

Squeegee. The rubber squeegee used for forcing the ink through the screen is mounted in a wooden handle. Blades are made in three grades: soft, medium and hard. For beginners the medium grade is ideal. The edge of the blade used for printing must be kept even and sharp.

Ink Screen-printing ink is available in four main types: Oil based; Cellulose based; Water based; Plastic based.

Beginners are recommended to use oil-based inks which can normally be thinned and cleaned from screens with inexpensive white spirit. Cellulose and plastic inks require special thinners and solvents. All thinners and solvents are highly inflammable and give off strong fumes which should not be inhaled. Adequate ventilation is, therefore, essential.

Printing surfaces. It is possible to print on almost any surface. Beginners should experiment with as wide a range of surfaces as possible. For cheap, experimental proof printing, newsprint paper is ideal. Finished prints on lithographic paper are excellent and these papers are available in a wide range of finishes.

Image-making; negative image-making; paper cuts. The simplest way of making an image for screen printing is to prepare a paper stencil which can be cut or torn into the required design. These paper cuts are ideal for one-colour prints. For more sophisticated prints, use one of the special hand-cut stencil papers such as Profilm or Stenplex which, when cut, are ironed on to the screen, making an excellent bond between the stencil and the printing screen.

Painted stencils. A stencil can be painted or drawn directly on to the screen using a filler, a water-soluble cellulose. Pronk, Davis and Rusby make a suitable filler called PDR Screen Filler. The filler should be used like paint. All the painted areas of the screen will, of course, resist the passage of the ink and the printed surface on the paper will comprise all the unpainted areas.

Negative/positive images; photographic stencils. It is possible to transfer a negative or positive image to screen by use of a photographic process. There are two methods both similar to the traditional way of making a photographic print. A negative image of an original can be made by transferring it on to a special transparent film, such as Ortholith or Gamma 4, which is an emulsion-coated surface capable of deep tones of black. Same-size images can be transferred by direct contact and enlargements or reductions can be made by using a special process camera. The film must be subsequently developed using specified chemicals and then attached to the screen. Positive images can be made by actually coating the surface of the screen with a light-sensitive photographic emulsion, such as Azocol, which is then allowed to dry. The coated screen must then be brought into firm contact with the negative image and exposed to a light source for a controlled period of time. In order to achieve complete contact between the original artwork and the prepared screen for both direct and film emulsion work, it may be necessary to place the artwork and the screen in a special vacuum exposure frame or sack which will enable all the air to be evacuated by means of an extractor valve and vacuum pump. Exposure to light hardens the emulsion on the screen that has received the image and the remainder of the emulsion can be washed away with warm water. After drying the screen is ready for printing. All manufacturers provide product information giving full details of these processes.

Printing. Ink is normally supplied in tins or tubes. Use a palette knife to transfer the ink to the taped inside edge of the screen. If the consistency of the ink is too thick to allow a smooth flow over the screen surface, then thin with an appropriate thinner.

Drying. After printing remove the print and place it on a drying rack separate from other prints. Screen-printing inks vary in their drying times. Oil-based inks tend to dry quickly, but other inks may take some time to become thoroughly dry.

Screen washing.   After processing, and when the screen is
required for a new image, all traces of inks and the original image must
be removed with a suitable screen wash such as Inksolve, Inkwash or
Deesolve. The manufacturer's instructions should be carefully
followed.

The simplest way of starting silk screen for the beginner is to buy a
ready prepared screen and some additional fabric from a supplier.
Reeves stock small printing frames ready fitted with an organdie fabric,
baseboard, adjustable bar and squeegee. It is also possible to obtain a
larger frame giving screen size of 535 × 305 mm. Organdie and
Polyester screen gauze is also available. Suppliers who stock Reeves's
products can usually also obtain Profilm for making self-adhesive paper
stencils, staple guns, staples for fixing the fabric to the screen, gummed
paper strip, in rolls, for masking the edges of the frame and squeegees.
Sericol and Pronk, Davis and Rusby are major suppliers of screen inks
and related materials and suppliers who stock Reeves's products can
obtain Colourjet screen inks in a choice of ten colours, with black and
white. Product information sheets are available giving full details of the
properties and use of inks.

An example of a silk-screen print is given in Fig. 1.11.

Lithography

The lithographic print process is one of the most popular print-making
methods and is capable of printing both direct and photographic images
by reverse printing★ or offset printing.★ The process relies on the
natural tendency of grease, contained in the drawing material, to repel
water. Any greasy mark made on a lithographic plate is capable of being
printed, but special drawing materials are normally used. There are two
basic types of lithographic printing. The *direct method* produces a
reverse image and the *offset method* produces a positive image. The
direct method involves the transfer of an image to a zinc, aluminium or
plastic plate by direct drawing on the plate, transferring a drawing from
a transparency or photographic transfer. The offset method produces
positive images by transferring the image from the plate to a special
roller during the printing process which subsequently prints a positive
image on the paper.

The plates
Lithographic plates are grained by the manufacturer to produce a
surface which is capable of taking greasy substances such as inks,
chalks and crayons which naturally resist water. This graining is not
easily apparent to the eye or to the touch. Zinc plates must usually be
treated before use to remove oxide coating. This can be done by using a
special solution such as Preposal and then rinsing the plate in water.
The grain of the plate can vary according to the type of work, with fine
grain being used for plates which take photographic images. A

Fig. 1.11 Silk-screen print – 'The Beach Boys' (1964) by Peter Blake

lithographic plate can only be used for one image and one colour: an additional plate is required for every additional colour.

Image-making
The simplest way to make an image is to draw, with special ink, chalk or crayon, directly on to the surface of the plate. Litho ink is normally supplied in bars which need melting either in water, preferably distilled, or turpentine, until the required consistency is reached. Litho chalks and crayons are available in a range of hardness from soft 00 to

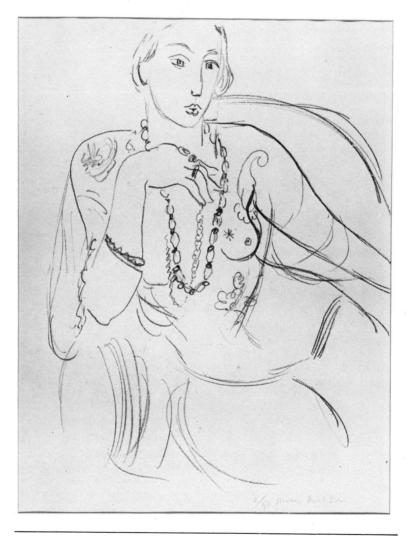

Fig. 1.12   Lithograph by Henri Matisse (1869–1954)

hard No. 5. Alternatively, the image can first be drawn on a special transparent plastic film, which is capable of taking ink or pencil images, such as UNO matt drafting film. If more than one colour is to be used on the final print a separate image is required for each coloured area. Photo-opaque can also be used for drawing and correcting images or used as a completely opaque medium. Black crayons and waterproof drawing ink can also be used on transparent film. Colour work is simplified by using transparent sheets for all the drawing stages. A master drawing, in full colour, should be completed and overlays of transparent film used to isolate each colour area for the printing process. As each stage is completed, it is necessary to place corresponding registration marks on each sheet to ensure that all the overlays match on the final print. A more sophisticated method of colour separation can be obtained using photo-mechanical processes which ensure accurate registration, and these methods can be used with any printmaking method.

Inks
Lithographic inks are capable of being thinned to make excellent transparent colours and this enables a very wide range of tones to be achieved. Each colour to be printed requires a separate plate and, to ensure correct superimposition of the colours on the final print, it is usual to mark each plate with an identical registration mark (+) in each corner. However, the number of plates required is affected by the choice of colours and the sequence in which they are printed. For example, a blue printed over a yellow will produce a green. When planning the printing of colours it is essential to try and achieve the maximum use of colour with the minimum number of plates.

Photographic images
Line, half-tone* and continuous tone images can be reproduced on lithographic plates. Continuous tone images must first be processed using a dot screen to break up the image into a series of dots like the method used for producing newspaper photographs. The image is then transferred to a plate which has been treated with a light-sensitive photographic emulsion. Exposure to light hardens the drawn image and the remaining emulsion can then be washed off. Hunter Penrose Ltd are major suppliers of lithographic materials.

A lithograph by Matisse is shown in Fig. 1.12.

CHAPTER 2

Specialisms in art and design

It is possible to start a specialist course in one of the design areas from the age of sixteen by attending one of the full-time or part-time BTEC (DATEC) design courses. Many students, however, prefer to join a more general diagnostic course after leaving school and before deciding on their final choice of specialist study, and these students would expect to start specialisation at the age of eighteen. There are six major areas of design work and several minor areas. Full details are given in the reference section of the courses that are available. Each area has its own work methods and professional practices and, with the exception of fine art, its own career structure. Several of the areas overlap and it is often possible to work in two or more related areas. Some of the work such as Product Design requires a multi-disciplinary training, and other areas are very highly specialised such as medical photography or scientific illustration. Although fine art does not provide for a career, many fine artists find employment in related activities which demand the use of creative ideas.

In some design areas it is possible to work with relatively limited resources or as a free-lance designer with a small studio or workshop. These areas can include ceramics, jewellery, silversmithing, fashion design, textile design and graphic design, and the sections of this part of the book dealing with these subjects include some basic information on materials and methods to indicate the nature of the activities.

2.1. GRAPHIC DESIGN

The description 'graphic designer' is an all-embracing term for a person whose job is mainly the design of printed material, particularly for the advertising industry. Designers can, however, be specialists in one or more areas, including typography, packaging, all types of illustration, television and film graphics, book design, layout, stamp design, logos★, liveries, house styles★ and audio-visual presentations. The graphic designer is involved with the creative, economically viable presentation of words and images so that they achieve their maximum effect.

Normally a designer works to a brief set by a client which may outline the nature of the task, the financial limitations, the market for which the product is aimed and possibly the concept that the designer has to project. Sometimes a designer is responsible for the total house style of a company or institution or the promotion of a product such as a perfume or a brand of petrol, but often a team is given the task under the supervision of an art director who will bring together other specialists such as copywriters and photographers. Designers must be aware of ethical, social and legal restraints and be familiar with typography and printing methods and photography. Draughtsmanship and drawing skills are essential. Above all the designer must have creative ability and the professional expertise to translate ideas into visual images.

The design process

Before starting the detailed work on a design, the designer must obtain as much information as possible about the needs of the client. The most appropriate method of reproduction must be chosen and the size of the finished design established. In some cases, such as the column width of a newspaper or the size of a railcard for an underground train this will be predetermined. If colour can be used, the designer must decide how it is to be used. Sometimes a particular type of paper might need to be chosen and this could be influenced by cost and the choice of printing process. The actual words to be used, known as the copy, their emphasis in the design and the choice of appropriate type styles and sizes must be decided and a decision on the possible use of photographs or illustrations might be made. Once decisions have been reached on such basic points, the designer is ready to proceed to the layout.

Employment for designers tends to be either in a studio, which is usually a fairly small, independent specialist firm possibly servicing several larger firms, or in an agency which can be a large international company dealing with a number of major clients. The influence of the work of the graphic designer can be seen everywhere from postage stamps to Guinness posters. Much of the work has a short life and the industry therefore tends to consume large numbers of creative ideas over relatively short periods of time.

Layout: scamps/roughs

Initial ideas, possibly noted in pencil on scraps of paper are known as *scamps*. Such ideas, often from several sources, are brought together by the designer who is to plan the layout. This involves producing a number of alternative designs called *roughs*, usually on layout paper using feltmarkers. The roughs enable the designer to experiment with various ways of dividing the space required for text and pictorial areas and establish any margins or grids that may be required. Eventually the final version of the layout will be produced, often in consultation with the client, and this is known as a *finished rough*. It will indicate the final positions of all the components of the design.

Grids: modular design

Pre-printed grid sheets are now normally provided for any publication which follows a standard format for more than one issue, such as magazines, and also for book production. The example shown of a grid sheet in Fig. 2.1 is the Longman standard text grid sheet showing the layout of this page, and Fig. 2.2 is another example from this book of how authors set out their ideas for the book designer. The designer can vary the amount of text or the size of the illustrations in relation to the grid. The grid can show the column widths of text and also margins and can be given either horizontal or vertical emphasis.

Dry transfer lettering

These are hand-lettering methods using transferable type prepared on plastic-backed sheets or transfer cards. The characters are transferred by hand pressure using a blunt tool or special spatula. A large range of symbols is also available. Graphic designers find useful the co-ordinated lines and dots, points, graduated tints, borders and rules which are available on transfer sheets. Self-adhesive coloured films and papers are other design aids and, for sign-writing or similar work, PVC transfer lettering can be used on surfaces such as glass, metal, plaster and painted wood.

Typography

All graphic designers need to have a thorough knowledge of typography and it is possible to specialise in this subject. Designers are responsible for the selection of a suitable typeface for a particular job and this depends on a number of things, including the nature of the work, the designer's style, the client's requirements and the printing methods. There are hundreds of typefaces available and new ones are being designed each year. Besides being available in roman and italic, each typeface usually includes a number of variations of style and size. Type variations can be in condensed or extended forms and are often available in different weights such as light face, medium face, or bold face. The small decorative strokes usually shown at the top or bottom of a letter are called serifs, and 'sans serif' simply means 'without serif'. Recognition of typefaces, for example Univers or Helvetica, is made visually, and can only be achieved after long practice. However, there are recognition aids available for the beginner, in the form of printed sheets of various typefaces and sizes available from the Monotype Corporation or other suppliers. Typefaces are also referred to by series numbers, for example 'Times Roman 327'. In typesetting specifications it is usual to specify both the name of the typeface and the series number.

Composition methods – printing

There are two typesetting composition processes.

Hot metal process

This is the traditional letterpress printing method involving the production of metal lines of type. The most well-known of such setting systems are the Linotype and the Monotype. The Linotype is a single-machine system which composes type in a solid line (a 'slug') to a predetermined measure. Any corrections to a line means that the line has to be reset. The typesetting is initiated by using a large keyboard.

The Monotype system is a dual-machine system comprising a typesetting keyboard and a type-casting machine. The combination of these produces lines of type cast to predetermined measure, with each letter of the line being a separate piece of type. Corrections to a line of setting can be done by hand, the line being justified to its original measure.

Photo-composition

Photo-typesetting is a more economical method for type composition. The process is keyboard activated and produces text ready set as a photo-negative or as a positive print from which can be developed the printing plate. Photo-typesetting machines use a computer or micro-processor to translate the input from the keyboard, select the correct typeface and print size and store the copy. The operator, who can also be the designer, can see the composition of the text develop on a visual display unit (VDU) as the copy is typed into the machine and corrections can be made during this stage. The introduction of these compact machines into design studios enables designers to work directly with the actual copy that eventually forms the printed page. Photo-composition is also used for the production of 'display' type. The storage of information is by either magnetic tape or floppy disk.* The machines have large storage capacities and one disk can store hundreds of thousands of characters. Text that has been processed by a photo-typesetting machine is described as *filmset*.

Micro-processors

The development of technology using micro-processors enables the graphic designer and the typographic designer to produce images in either black and white or colour by use of a digitising pad, an electronic pencil and an appropriate software* program. The results can be instantly seen on a VDU and, if required, they can be printed and incorporated into layouts. Organisations such as the BBC are using

The actual words to be used, known as the copy, their emphasis
in the design and the choice of appropriate type styles and sizes
must be decided and a decision on the possible use of photographs
or illustrations might be made. Once decisions have been reached
on such basic points the designer is ready to proceed to the layout.

Employment for designers tends to be either in a studio, which is
usually a fairly small, independent specialist firm possibly servicing several larger firms or in an agency which can be a large
international company dealing with a number of major clients. The
influence of the work of the graphic designer can be seen everywhere
from postage stamps to Guinness posters. Much of the work has a
short life and the industry therefore tends to consume large numbers
of creative ideas over relatively short periods of time.

Layout: Scamps/Roughs. Initial ideas, possibly noted in pencil on
scraps of paper are known as Scamps. Such ideas, often from several
sources, are brought together by the designer who is to plan the layout. This involves producing a number of alternative designs called Roughs, usually on layout paper using felt markers. The Roughs
enable the designer to experiment with various ways of dividing the
space required for text and pictorial areas and establish any margins or grids that may be required. Eventually the final version
of the layout will be produced, often in consultation with the client,
and this is known as a Finished Rough. It will indicate the final
positions of all the components of the design. Grids/Modular
Design. Pre-printed grid sheets are now normally provided for any
publication which follows a standard format for more than one issue
such as magazines and also for book production.

Insert figure 2.1

The example shown of a grid sheet in Fig. 2.1 is the Longman stan-

---

Fig. 2.1   Longman standard text grid sheet with prepared text

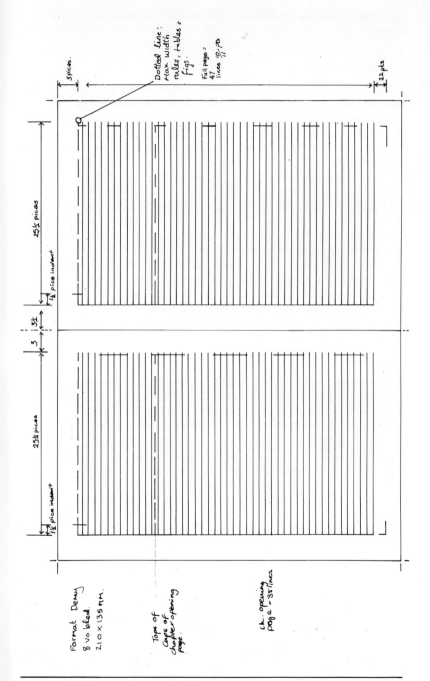

Fig. 2.2   Page layout for this handbook.

electronic character generators to produce a wide range of graphic images.

Copyfitting

When large areas of text have to be specified, the designer has to ensure that the available space will accommodate the required number of characters. This process is called 'copyfitting'. Type scales, which resemble rulers, are useful in measuring the width of a typesetting and, for small areas of type, a character count is a reasonably accurate measure of indication as to whether the print size chosen is likely to fit the space available on the page. The designer is helped by working from a typed script which is usually set in either an élite typeface, with twelve characters to the inch, or in a pica face, with ten characters to the inch. If, however, there is a lot of copy to be fitted, then a standard copyfitting table can be used to decide the number of characters for the space available in the layout.

Experimentation with type is essential for the beginner, and hand-lettering is a useful method of becoming familiar with letter forms. The spacing between characters is important. Serif characters, for example, do not all occupy the same amount of space on the printed page. A study of typefaces is a useful introduction to typography.

Illustration

There are two main types of illustration work. *Technical illustration*, which is a highly specialised method of technical drawing, and *general illustration*, which includes book, magazine, film and television illustration. Illustrators are generally self-employed and work as free-lance illustrators or as author/illustrators on, for example, children's books. Technical illustrators are concerned with the illustration of technical processes and machinery and sometimes specialise in aeronautical, electrical or mechanical engineering illustration. Most illustrators use similar tools for producing their work, but general illustrators are sometimes involved in print processes which are craft-based, such as wood engraving or etching. An airbrush is a useful tool combining compressed air and colour to produce a fine, controllable spray through a special, pen-shaped tool. DeVilbiss airbrushes are very good and for beginners the 'Sprite' is ideal. It includes a plastic cup which has a capacity of 5 cc, but for spraying large areas the 'Sprite Major' is fitted with a colour container with a capacity of 28.4 ml. For occasional use the best way to obtain the necessary supply of compressed air is from an aerosol. The airbrush hose should be fitted with a special control valve which can easily be connected to the top of the can. Speedry Magic Marker Airbrush Propellant is ideal and is supplied in twin packs containing two 20 oz aerosols. The same firm market Magic Colour, a range of twelve colours specially prepared for airbrush work. The art of airbrushing relies on effective masking and Magic Marker have also developed a masking film available in rolls and A2, A3 and A4 sheet sizes.

Illustrators need to be familiar with typography and the whole range of image-producing processes. Photography is a very valuable resource and film can be used as a method of visually recording information required for illustrations or combining photographic techniques with traditional illustrative work. Some illustrators specialise in animation work using a film camera which is combined with a special camera mount with both a movable carriage and a baseboard.

Technical illustrators need high standards of numeracy as much of their work requires very accurate detailed drawing to scale.

Artwork

The final stage in the presentation of a design is the preparation of all the materials required for printing, possibly including text, photographs, line drawings, illustrations and colour separations. This is called the *artwork*. This is sometimes done by the designer and sometimes by other specialists. The artwork can be assembled to the designer's instructions in a positive form ready to be photographed or as a photo-negative on film ready to be transferred to the printing plate. If the artwork is to be produced with positive material the text may have already been typeset and will be positioned in the final layout as appropriate. The process of assembling artwork is known as *paste up* and specialist paste-up artists are employed to carry out this work in some firms.

Television

Graphic designers who work in television are responsible for the design and supervised execution of title sequences, credits and all programme material of a graphic nature. The recruitment is generally from applicants who have successfully completed a BA or equivalent level course in an appropriate subject. Graphic design assistants must also have had previous successful training to BA or equivalent level and some experience in advertising or related industries is an advantage. Design assistants work, under supervision, with graphic designers and holiday relief vacancies sometimes occur at the BBC. A most important requirement is good draughtsmanship.

Graphic assistants

The staff who work in the Graphic Design Print Room at the BBC are known as graphic assistants. They produce a wide variety of typographic material for film and television productions. The work includes credit captions and small graphic properties of all kinds, and the production methods include advanced electronic character generators. Experience in letter assembly and typing is desirable. Accuracy in the presentation of work is essential and an art school training is an advantage.

2.2 PHOTOGRAPHY/FILM/TELEVISION

Photography

Work in this area has close links with a number of other professions including journalism, advertising and fashion. There is also the area of scientific and technical photography. All art and design students should own and use a camera, preferably one with interchangeable lenses. Ideal are 35 mm reflex cameras which enable the actual image to be viewed through the lens, and excellent cameras are available from reputable second-hand camera dealers. It is always worthwhile purchasing a camera case for the protection of the camera and, for expensive cameras, it may be advisable to insure them against loss.

The relationship between the photographer and the artist and designer can be a working partnership or the roles can be combined where the artist/designer/photographer is one person, undertaking all aspects of the work.

Creative photography

This category includes artist/photographers who use the medium to promote their philosophical and social ideas in visual terms and includes some aspects of experimental photography. Sometimes artists, such as R. B. Kitaj, Andy Warhol and Robert Rauschenberg, have used photography as part of their creative work and some American painters, such as Don Eddy, Richard Estes and Richard McLean, have used photographs as the source material for their paintings. Creative photography also includes the work of photographers who explore aspects of the visual world in photographic terms, such as Richard Avedon, Bill Brandt and Snowdon. This group belongs to one of the oldest traditions of the medium, going back to the early pioneers, such as Margaret Cameron.

Specialist photography

The most famous of this group are the fashion photographers, such as David Bailey, but this area also includes the specialists who work in laboratories and hospitals or with the police.

Photo-journalists

This is possibly the largest group of professional photographers, who either work as employees for national and regional newspapers or as free-lance photographers for newspapers and magazines.

There is some overlap between all these areas, and a photographer may work in two or more areas. However, the personal reputation of a professional photographer is often built on the quality of image-making relating to a small area of specialisation.

Materials

Kodak make a range of chemicals suitable for the beginner who wishes to experiment. Their Universal Developer is a highly concentrated, all-purpose liquid suitable for both film (negatives) and papers. It is available in 500 ml and 5-litre sizes. The Kodal Indicator Stop Bath arrests development immediately and is economical. It minimises 'fog' and removes scum which can occur during the development stage. When exhausted the stop bath turns purple. Available in 1-litre containers. Kodafix solution is a rapid-hardening fixer, also suitable for films and papers, fast working and economical. Available in both 500 ml and 5-litre sizes.

Papers: contrast grades – Kodak papers

0. Extra soft contrast. This grade is particularly suitable for negatives of very high contrast.
1. Soft. This grade is suitable for high-contrast negatives.
2. Normal. Particularly suitable for negatives of medium contrast.
3. Hard. This grade is suitable for low-contrast negatives.
4. Extra hard. A grade for negatives of very low contrast.

The Kodachrome 11 RC Paper Type 2450 is a continuous-tone, black-and-white, resin-coated enlarging paper suitable for contact prints, photograms and projected enlargements. It is available with two surfaces, 'F' – glossy, in six contrast grades from 0 to 5, and 'N' – semi-matt, in four contrast grades from 1 to 4.

Colour processing

It is possible to carry out colour processing with fairly limited facilities, but automatic commercial printing methods are very competitive in price and may make the purchase of the necessary equipment and chemicals uneconomic. For experimental work, however, it is very useful to have a simple colour-printing system available.

Colour prints can also be produced using special films and cameras such as those manufactured by Polaroid and Kodak. The size of the original print is limited, but commercially produced enlargements are possible. No additional chemicals are required to produce the original image. The special film contains the necessary processing chemicals and the manufacturer's instructions should be closely followed.

Lighting

It is often necessary to provide special lighting for photographic work and specialist publications give full details of the wide range of equipment available and its suitability for different types of work. A simple flash unit, preferably attached to the camera, may be necessary if photographs are to be taken in poor lighting conditions such as museums. Flash cubes enable a number of exposures to be made using one cube. Electronic flash units are capable of a large number of exposures under controlled lighting conditions and these units can be battery/mains operated.

Experimental photography

Experiments are most important for beginners whose previous experience of photography may have been limited. A good starting-point is a simple photogram made by placing thin, two-dimensional objects in the film holder on the enlarger or using larger, three-dimensional objects placed directly on the enlarger baseboard. Combinations of these two methods are also possible and effective. No film negative is required. The enlarger lamp acts as the light source and, when the objects are placed directly in contact with the printing paper, the enlarger lens is not used. The results resemble silhouettes of the objects and effects of great subtlety can be achieved. The enlarger is used to create photographic images without the use of a camera.

Film sizes

Colour film is normally available in 110; 120; 126; 127; 135; 620 and 828 sizes with either 12; 20; 24 or 36 exposures per film. Black and white film is normally available in 110; 120; 126; 127; 135; 410; and 620 sizes with either 20 or 36 exposures per film.

Sheet film

The traditional sheet film sizes, quarter-plate, half-plate and whole-plate, are being replaced with the International range of 'A' sizes.

Film speed

The speed at which film is receptive to light is measured in DIN (Deutsche Industrie Norm), ASA (American Standards Association) and ISO (International Standards Organisation), all of whom provide calculations on which it is possible to correctly judge the exposure time required for films. The ASA/DIN/ISO number may need to be used both in connection with the camera setting and the setting of an exposure meter. The higher the number, the faster the film.

Colour film: negative film for colour negatives/colour prints

Kodacolor II: General-purpose colour negative film, medium speed for daylight use with either electronic flash or blue flashbulbs. High sharpness, ultra-fine grain and wide exposure latitude.

Kodacolor 400: High-speed, fine-grain colour film for dimly-lit and fast-action subjects and for work demanding high shutter speeds and small apertures. This film allows for greater flexibility in lighting conditions than Kodacolor II.

Films for colour slides

Kodak Ektachrome 64 (daylight): Medium-speed, general-purpose reversal film for daylight use with blue flashbulbs or electronic flash.

Kodak Ektachrome 160 (tungsten): Balanced for exposure by tungsten illumination.

Kodak Ektachrome 200 (daylight): High-speed film for fast action, interiors lighted by daylight, floodlit buildings and other subjects in dim lighting conditions where it is not possible or desirable to use a flash.

Kodak Ektachrome 400 (daylight): Very high-speed colour reversal film for use in dim lighting conditions and particularly useful for hand-held exposures.

Kodachrome 25 (daylight): An extremely fine-grain colour slide film of high resolving power and sharpness, combined with superb colour rendering.

Kodachrome 64 (daylight): A medium-speed film, but faster than Kodachrome 25. High resolving power and sharpness.

Films for black and white prints

Kodak Panatomic-X film: A panchromatic film producing negatives with extremely fine grain and excellent definition. Useful for work under normal lighting conditions where very large prints are required. Use Kodak Microdol-X developer for processing.

Kodak Plus-X pan film: A versatile medium-speed film with many of the characteristics of Verichrome pan film. Suitable for work under a wide variety of lighting conditions. Process with Kodak Microdol-X developer.

Kodak Verichrome pan film: A general-purpose, medium-speed film capable of coping with a wide variety of lighting conditions. Process with Kodak Microdol-X.

Kodak Tri-X pan film: A high-speed, general-purpose film with fine grain, good resolving power and high sharpness. Particularly suitable for action photography, it has wide exposure and development latitude. Excellent degree of enlargement capability. Use Kodak D-76 developer powder for processing.

Kodak Recording Film 2475 (Estar-AH base): An extremely high-speed film with extended red sensitivity suitable for very low lighting levels and action subjects in poor light where it is not possible to use flash. Process with Kodak DK-50 developer powder.

Kodak Royal-X pan film: An extremely fast film of medium grain, normal contrast and wide exposure latitude, especially suitable for taking action pictures in extremely poor light. Process with Kodak DK-50 developer.

Kodak Panatomic-X and Plus-X films are available in 120 size as professional films.

Filters

A wide range of filters for general use on camera and enlarging lenses are made by Kodak under the trade name Wratten Filters. Each filter is designed for a particular use and many are capable of absorbing colours and ultraviolet radiation. Other filters include those which enable light intensity to be reduced by a definite ratio, and filters for lowering or raising the effective colour temperature of a light source.

Film and television training

The National Film School at Beaconsfield in Buckinghamshire provides full-time courses for students who wish to study for a professional career in film and/or television. The main criterion for entry is creative ability and there are no formal academic entry requirements. Entry is, effectively, by open competition and some students enter having recently completed university courses or courses at a similar level in an art and design college. The school, therefore, operates at the level of a postgraduate institution.

Four areas of activity are defined by the school, from which the student programme is drawn:

1. Technical or conceptual training in a workshop, either singly or as part of a group.
2. Screenings, discussions, lectures or seminars not related to specific production activities.
3. Personal or group production, including writing, or as a member of a crew on such a production.
4. Attachment to a professional production company.

A number of other colleges provide full-time courses leading to CNAA degrees in film and television, including the Polytechnic of Central London and Middlesex Polytechnic. The Royal College of Art provides a two- or three-year postgraduate (MA) course.

Some courses combine the study of photography with film and television, such as the London College of Printing Visual Communication Course, leading to a BA Honours degree, or the West Surrey College of Art and Design Photography, Film, Video and Animation Course, which also leads to a BA Honours degree: The course run jointly by Harrow College of Higher Education and Middlesex Polytechnic combines Applied Photography, Film and Television and includes the study of technical theory, aesthetics and sociology, leading to a BA Honours degree. Some Higher Diploma Visual Communications courses include Film/Television design.

2.3 FASHION DESIGN

The professional designing and construction of fashion garments, shoes, millinery and accessories is a very specialised activity. Students who wish to study for one of these areas normally first complete a DATEC Diploma (diagnostic) Course or a Foundation Course in Art and Design to confirm their choice of specialism or a DATEC Diploma or Certificate Course in a relevant specialised area. These courses can then be followed by Degree or DATEC Higher Diploma courses and postgraduate courses are also available. Mature students may be eligible for these courses or may join part-time City and Guilds courses, usually attending a college for one day per week.

Forecasting

A fashion designer can only work with the colour ranges and cloths that are available. Their availability depends, to a certain extent, on accurate forecasting of fashion trends. A number of organisations and individual designers carry out forecasting to help cloth manufacturers plan their production. In Europe one of the main forecasting systems is that carried out by organisations closely associated with the production and promotion of specific cloths such as the International Institute for Cotton and the International Wool Secretariat. Meetings of such organisations take place about eighteen months before the garments are required in the shops and result in forecasts of colour and design trends being passed to cloth manufacturers. Forecasting relies on a sensitive response to possible influences and can include social trends, the effects of changes in popular culture, films, television and major international exhibitions. Without efficient planning it would be impossible for manufacturers to cater for the international mass market, as they need time to plan their production, which can involve manufacturing millions of metres of cloth for a major change in fashion styles. The major forecasting organisations have forecasting rooms containing samples of the proposed new cloths and colour schemes and where trade representatives can see the ideas proposed for forthcoming seasons.

The design process

The designer usually starts the planning of a new range of garments by choosing fabrics and colour schemes for possible translation into clothes. The choice of materials is sometimes influenced by a personal forecast of fashion trends. The particular concept for a new style is seldom based on the personal needs of the designer. Such concepts are more likely to be affected by the availability of cloths and the possible demands of particular age, social and economic groups of the people who are to buy and wear the clothes. Having chosen a range of fabrics and colours, the designer sketches possible alternative variations of styles, ensuring that the finished sketches are capable, if necessary, of being translated, by mass-production techniques of manufacture, into identical copies of the original design in a range of sizes. To enable designers to work systematically, the actual designing can either be carried out on blocks, which are permanent records on card of standard body sizes, or by making up a garment from a cheap fabric directly on to a dress stand of the appropriate size. Designs which are made up in this way are called *toiles*. In both cases the design has finally to be translated into a paper pattern and a skilled technician called a grader is required later to adjust the pattern according to the sizes required for the production garments. A standard block for women's clothes normally consists of five pieces:

1. Front bodice;
2. Back bodice;
3. Sleeve;
4. Front skirt;
5. Back skirt.

The designer adjusts the block or the toile to suit the new style, and the paper pattern, which is then cut, reflects the nature and style of the new garment, including additions such as collars or extra seams. Both blocks and stands can change their proportions and shape according to the prevalent fashion style. An Edwardian block, for example, is quite different from a 1980s block, and similarly with the shape of stands. The majority of commercial patterns are planned on blocks, and are therefore cut flat. After the cutting of the fabric, which is another skilled craft, undertaken by trained pattern cutters, the pieces of cloth are made up into a sample garment by a skilled machinist. Large manufacturers often have a sample room which is set aside for the production of 'one-off' garments so that they can be approved before being mass-produced in the clothing factory. Computer programs are now available which will undertake the cutting of fabric, and the development of micro-processors is also having an influence on production methods.

Theatre costume design

Although the work of a theatre costume designer is similar in many ways to that of the fashion designer, the nature of work for opera-houses, television and film studios and theatres requires a special interest and ability to design original or historical costumes, often using materials and methods which are a simulation of the real thing. Career opportunities are limited. Some designers who work in this area qualified as fashion designers and subsequently specialised, while others have completed a professional course of training in theatre costume design. Like stage designers, costume designers have to work as part of

Fig. 2.3   Fashion illustration – Advanced Diploma in Fashion Course student –
Barnet College

a team, usually under the direction of a theatre director. In some cases a production director will co-ordinate the design of the lighting, staging and costumes for a production, particularly if the resources are extensive, such as for an opera. In such cases the influence of the costume designer could be minimal and limited to interpretations of the creative ideas of other people. Costume designers who work in large theatrical, opera or ballet companies will often have the resources of workshops and specialist staff. The attributes of the fashion designer, combined with an innovative flair for improvisation, are a good background for this kind of work.

Fashion illustration

This is a specialised area of illustration and is usually done by trained fashion designers who have the necessary creative drawing ability. Most fashion design courses include illustration as part of the programme of study. Employment opportunities are limited to free-lance work and there are close associations with fashion journalism.
A fashion illustration is shown in Fig. 2.3.

Footwear design

The design of boots and shoes for men, women and children is another specialised design activity and training can start from the age of sixteen years on DATEC courses. There are, however, very few centres as career opportunities are limited. Some fashion courses include the design of footwear in their syllabuses and specialist courses are provided by the Cordwainers' Technical College in London, which provides vocational courses up to production management level. Leicester Polytechnic provides a CNAA degree course in footwear at both BA and MA levels.

2.4 TEXTILE DESIGN

Textile designers usually specialise in either printed, knitted or woven fabrics. With printed fabrics the design is imposed on the material by one of several alternative printing processes, of which screen (flat bed or gravure), heat transfer (Sublastic – trade name for transfer paper printing process using heat) or spray are the most common, depending on the type of fabric. Knitted and woven fabrics incorporate the design as part of the manufacturing process. A number of designer/crafts people combine the roles of designer and manufacturer by specialising in the printing or painting of individual fabrics by hand or in hand-knitting or hand-loom weaving. Constructed textiles combine two or more processes. Industrial manufacturing in the United Kingdom has been adversely affected by foreign competition particularly from the Far East and, for some fashion areas, from Italy. Much design work, however, is still carried out by British designers who may work as free-lance designers for several manufacturers or market their designs through agents in the USA, Europe or Japan. Designers also work as staff designers for individual firms, possibly producing a 'house style', while others work for design groups or studios for joint marketing and exhibition purposes.

Fabrics vary according to their use which can include menswear, women's wear, furnishing (domestic and contract) and specialist, which can include such items as fabrics for aircraft, train and car seats. The largest design areas are possibly for fashion and household textiles. The nature of the fashion industry, with its emphasis on changing styles and seasonal collections, can involve the designer with a large turnover of designs from year to year, but the furnishing industry is traditionally conservative, although some areas such as household linens, curtain fabrics and co-ordinated schemes can involve a designer in responding to fashion trends. There are three basic textile printing methods suitable for beginners:

1. Relief printing;
2. Screen printing;
3. Resist printing.

Relief printing

Block printing is a relief-printing process similar to the woodcut printing methods used by print-makers. The design is first traced and then transferred to the surface of the wood block by placing the tracing face down and burnishing it from the back. The areas of the block to be printed in colour are then painted in a water-soluble paint and cutting tools used to remove all the unpainted areas of wood. Fabric printing blocks are generally cut deeper than woodcut blocks as fabric is less resilient than paper to pressure. Although this method is ideal for simple, one-colour designs, multicoloured prints can best be printed using a wood block with a felt inlay to absorb and evenly distribute the colour to the fabric. A separate block is required for each colour. Metal strips can also be used to make intricate patterns. The strips are hammered into the softwood block to produce a thin, metal edge which becomes the printing surface. Registration marks for multicoloured work are essential and are made by inserting brass pins, known as pitch pins, in the corners of the block.

A firm, stable printing table is required. The table should be covered with a thick woollen blanket which must be completely encased in a waterproof sheet such as Neoprene. Over this should be stretched a smooth, plain cotton fabric backing cloth which stops the ink from marking the waterproof cover. The fabric to be printed should be pinned to the cloth at intervals, depending on the type of fabric, to prevent movement.

Screen printing

The basic techniques for textile screen printing are similar to those for print-making on paper. Metal frames are generally used because they are lighter than wood and more easily handled and they do not warp when wetted for cleaning. The fabric is fixed to the screen with adhesive lacquer covering the face side of the frame. The warp and weft of the fabric is placed parallel to the sides of the frame. Screen-printing tables need to be longer than those required for block printing as the area of the screen is considerably larger than a normal wood block. The table should be prepared in the same way, however, with the addition of a suitable registration rail and stops placed exactly parallel to the outside edge of the print table. This will enable the screen to be fixed accurately to the printing surface and the registration angle bar on the screen will enable it to be keyed into the appropriate stop point. The stop points are placed at the distance apart of the exact 'drop' of the repeat. The whole width of the cloth is printed at one time using one screen for each colour. The length of fabric to be printed is subdivided into units and numbers one, three and five, etc. are usually printed first and allowed to dry, followed by numbers two, four and six, etc. which prevents 'marking off' on the underside of the screen. Squeegee blades need to be hard and the edges are usually V-shaped.

Colour separations, if required, are usually prepared by hand, using Kodatrace and photographic opaque. Photo-mechanical separations are sometimes necessary when particularly difficult photographic imagery is being used or if a detailed trichromatic separation* is required. The mesh size of the screen is important. The number of threads to the square centimetre chosen for a particular screen depends on the nature of the artwork. Textile meshes can usually be slightly coarser than those required for graphic prints because the image is often of a larger size.

Resist printing

Batik is a method of resist fabric printing which originated in Java (Indonesia). It is based on the ability of wax to resist cold water and uses brushes and a traditional tool called a *tjanting* to draw designs in liquid wax directly on to a fabric from which all artificial dressing has been removed. The fabric can be waxed and dyed several times in more than one colour and, when completed, the wax can be removed by boiling the fabric in water.

Tie-dyeing is another resist method which utilises tied knots, sewn threads and the incorporation of small stones and pebbles held into the

fabric by elastic bands or threads to resist cold-water dyes. The fabric
can be dyed in several colours or in several tones of the same colour,
removing, after each dyeing, a section of the tied, sewn or knotted
design. It is also possible to add new elements to the design at any
stage. Batik and tie-dyeing methods can be combined in the design of
the same fabric, and the traditional colour for tie-dyed fabric is indigo.

Repeating patterns

The production of repeats in design work for fashion fabrics is not
usually required and the drawing based on the original idea, known as a
croquis, after the French word meaning an outline, is usually sold not in
repeat. A designer will normally charge an additional fee if a repeat is
required. Designs for furnishing fabrics, however, are normally sold in
repeat. The number of designs in a collection often determines the
amount of time spent on repeat work. When fashion and furnishing
fabrics are similar, both in imagery and style, repeat work can be a
positive disadvantage. There are a number of types of repeats of which
the most common are block, brick, interlocking, half-drop (mirror
vertical, mirror horizontal and mirror diagonal), turn about, foulard
and various spot repeats. Examples of repeat patterns are shown in Fig.
2.4.

Textile printing colours and dyestuffs

Dyes require different methods of application for different types of
fabrics and also have special characteristics. Some dyes completely
permeate cloth while others do not permeate at all or only partly
permeate. Paints, inks and crayons are available for working directly on
to fabrics. The imagery conceived for a print often dictates the print
method to be used and also the type of fabric.

Suppliers

T. N. Lawrence can supply wood blocks and the necessary cutting
tools and inks. Pronk, Davis and Rusby and Selectasine Serigraphics
specialise in other materials and equipment.

Weaving

There are three basic weaves used for the production of cloth:
1. *Plain weave*: Producing a fabric which is lightweight, reversible,
   firmly constructed and durable.
2. *Twill weave*: A variation of plain weave using more warp than weft
   when the cloth is to be warp faced and more weft yarns when a
   weft face is required. A diagonal weave is produced across the
   cloth.

Block Repeat

Brick Repeat

Half-drop

Mirror Vertical half-drop

Mirror Horizontal

Interlocking

Fig. 2.4   Repeating patterns by a student on the DATEC General Art and Design diploma course at Barnet College

3. *Satin weave*: This uses long warp yarns which pass over a number of weft yarns before passing under a weft yarn. Generally, this weave produces a lustre to the surface, but it has poorer durability than plain or twill weave.

There are two main types of yarn used for weaving in wool: woollen yarn and worsted yarn. Woollen yarn, when made up into woven cloth, has a bulky, fuzzy texture and is produced from yarns in which the individual fibres come together in a random way. Worsted yarn produces woven cloth which has a smooth texture and is more durable than woollen cloth. This yarn is composed of long fibres of wool which are parallel.

Cotton, silk, flax and man-made fibres are also extensively used, either individually or in mixtures, as yarns for weaving.

Knitted fabrics

Machine knitting

The machine process for manufacturing knitwear is similar to plain or stocking stitch knitting by hand. The yarn is machine-knitted into a series of horizontal rows or loops called *courses* and, as the process continues, vertical rows of loops are formed known as *wales*. The term 'fully fashioned knitwear' refers to a process where the shape of the garment is determined by the machine increasing or decreasing the number stitches and forming the shape of the finished garment. When the required shape is cut from a knitted length of fabric the process is known as 'cut and sew' knitwear. Changes in the structure of knitwear fabrics are achieved by using different-sized needles. Some knitted fabrics have an elastic quality and the appearance of horizontal or vertical ribbed lines.

The most common form of knitting machine is a flat bed which carries the yarn backwards and forwards along a row of needles. These machines can be either power- or hand-operated. Some machines can provide for the introduction of unspun fibres, thus allowing the making of fabrics with a soft, deep pile, and these machines also incorporate a carding unit which can produce parallel fibres for incorporation into the yarn. Warp knitting machines knit together yarns from the warp and this method is used to produce very open-weave fabrics.

Hand knitting

Woollen, worsted, cotton, man-made and blended yarns are available for hand knitting. The majority of yarns are composed of two or more yarns twisted together and known as *multiple-ply yarns*. The greater the number of yarns the thicker the ply. Effective hand knitting relies on the correct tension being maintained and this is affected by the size of needles used. If the tension is too loose, smaller needles are required and, where the tension is too tight, larger needles are needed.

Surface pattern design

This is an area of design related to textiles, but normally dealing with pattern designing on materials and products other than textiles. This includes designing for wallcoverings, giftwraps, decorated consumer products (such as tins, trays and mugs), ceramics, laminates, tiles, paper cups, plates, napkins and other products which incorporate surface patterns. Co-ordinated designs, where one pattern is used on a wide range of products, maximise the potential point-of-sale outlets and markets. The largest area of co-ordinated design is probably household textiles where one pattern can be repeated on curtains, bed linen, upholstery, table linen, cushion covers, lampshades and floor rugs.

The range of materials can vary from chintz cottons to PVC fabrics and from ceramic tiles for the bathroom to plastic mugs for the kitchen. There are specialist courses in surface pattern design and several textile design courses include this area of work in their syllabuses.

2.5 THREE-DIMENSIONAL DESIGN

This area of work encompasses the largest group of design activities, ranging from the self-employed designer/craftsman to the industrially based designer working as a member of a team for a mass-production industry. One unifying factor is the necessity for all those concerned with these activities to have a developed awareness, creativity and ability for dealing with design problems involving space, volume, form and decoration. Many aspects of three-dimensional design also require the ability to make accurate mathematical calculations and to work to fine degrees of measurement. Numeracy is, therefore, most important. All areas require skill in handling tools and a knowledge of the characteristics of a wide range of materials.

A number of courses are available which offer a broad general introduction to certain specific areas of work and then provide an opportunity to specialise in one or more chief study. Other courses concentrate on specific design areas such as ceramics, while some offer a programme of study which is an amalgam, for example wood/metal/ceramics/plastics.

Ceramics

Ceramics is one of the oldest recorded crafts in the world and evidence of the work of potters has been found dating from thousands of years ago.

The majority of contemporary potters are self-employed or work as free-lance ceramic designers. The ceramics industry employs technicians and craftspeople as well as designers, but modern industrial methods of production offer relatively little opportunity for a career as a ceramic designer in full-time industrial employment. The relative simplicity of pottery methods, however, enables the beginner to learn the basic craft skills quickly and, if this craft ability is linked to creative design potential, then it is possible to develop a professional practice as a craft potter producing tableware and decorative pottery of all kinds. Some ceramic designers' work is non-utilitarian, producing 'fine-art' objects using a variety of methods and techniques.

Clay

The basic material for all pottery is clay, which is found in most parts of the world and chiefly consists of two main types, china clays, pure white and rather difficult for the beginner to use, and ball clays, which are available in Britain as either red (terracotta) or white clays, easy to use because of their ability to be easily shaped and moulded by hand. Ball clay is normally supplied either as prepared clay or as powdered clay which requires the addition of water to make it workable. The preparation of powdered clay is difficult for beginners with a limited amount of space and resources. It is possible to use local clays, particularly those dug from sites near river banks. Used clay can easily be reclaimed and reused, providing it has not been previously heated in a kiln, a process known as firing. All clays require firing in a kiln to make the clay objects durable.

Prepared clays are easily available for two types of hand-made pottery:
1. *Earthenware*: The most popular form of pottery for beginners. The clay objects have to be fired in a kiln to about 1100 °C, and this process gives them a smooth, slightly porous surface.
2. *Stoneware*: This pottery needs firing to a higher temperature than earthenware, needing between 1200 and 1350 °C. The resulting surface is non-porous and the objects will be stronger, but with limited possibilities for decoration.

The first firing of pottery in a kiln is known as a *biscuit* firing.

Tiles

It is sometimes difficult for beginners to make tiles which have an even thickness and regular shape. Variations caused by the qualities of the clay and the effects of drying and firing often cause warping and distortion to handmade tiles.

Moulds

Moulded dishes of all shapes and sizes can be simply made. Always try to design an original form on which to make the mould. There are two main types of mould: press moulds, where the dish shape is obtained by pressing the clay into a plaster of Paris mould, and hump moulds, where the dish shape is obtained by forming the clay over a moulded plaster form. Other pottery forms can be made by wrapping clay around a preformed shape of wood or similar material which has first been covered by newspaper to stop the clay adhering to the shape. Cylinder construction is particularly easy by this method.

Experiments

Always experiment with hand-making methods in order to explore the potential of clay as a means of creative expression. The plastic qualities of clay allow for a wide variety of treatment. Avoid stereotypes and repetitive designs copied from commercial ceramics. Use the basic construction methods to explore modelling possibilities. Visit the ceramic collections at the British Museum, the Victoria and Albert Museum, the Percival David Foundation in London and the provincial collections in centres such as Stoke-on-Trent, Cambridge, Oxford and Durham. Contemporary pottery of a high standard can often be seen at craft centres and at some art galleries.

Thrown pottery

The making of pottery forms by means of a revolving wheel is another traditional method of construction. Foot-operated (kick) wheels and electrically-operated wheels enable the potter to make a hollow pottery form by fashioning the clay as it revolves. Throwing pottery forms is usually easier for beginners on kick wheels, where greater control can be obtained. The process depends on accurate centring of the clay on the wheel before the thrown form can be developed. The ability to throw pots varies and some students find it impossible to achieve. It is only a part of pottery-making and, as plenty of other methods exist, the beginner should not be discouraged if unable successfully to use the wheel.

Decoration

Clay, in its plastic form before drying, can be decorated in a number of ways including pinching, fluting, indenting, incising and scratching. Such decoration then becomes part of the structure of the object.

Slip casting.   Pottery forms can also be decorated, before firing and when the clay is leather hard, by using a mixture of clay and water called 'slip'. It can be poured into dishes to form a decorative covering or used on pots by dipping them into a bucket of slip. It can also be used in a slip trailer, a nozzle fitted with a rubber, slip-filled bulb, which, when pressed, makes delicate patterns of slip on the clay.

Glazes

After the first (biscuit) firing in the kiln, pottery can be coated with a glaze made from silica and then fired in the kiln for a second time. This method will produce either a transparent or opaque glazed surface, depending on the nature of the materials. Ready-made glazes in powdered form are easily obtainable. A glaze is a mixture of silica and a flux, specially prepared for pottery, and, with experience, it is preferable to experiment and make individual glazes.

Kilns
It is not necessary to fire pottery only in an electric, gas or oil-fired kiln. Raku pottery, named after a form of Japanese pottery, uses an outdoor, hand-built kiln which can produce porous earthenware at a temperature of about 700 °C, fired by wood or a solid fuel such as coke. Small electric kilns are capable of glaze as well as biscuit firings, but may not be capable of reaching the temperatures required for stoneware. Oil- and gas-fired kilns are generally used only by the professional potter and are capable of the full range of process firings necessary for commercial production.

Kiln furniture
Fireproof kiln furniture for supporting the pottery in the kiln, such as shelves, known as bats, stilts and props, is specially made and the interior kiln temperatures can be indicated by pyromatic cones, known as Seger cones, which bend when specified temperatures are reached. The cones are placed in the kiln after the pottery has been packed and in a position where they can be observed, during the firing, through a peephole. More sophisticated kilns usually have a pyrometer attached to the outside of the kiln, linked with an interior kiln device which gives an accurate reading of the kiln temperature.

Damp cupboard
If it is necessary to retard the drying-out process of clay, for example if more work is required than can be achieved in one working session, then the clay object should be wrapped in polythene and kept in a moist atmosphere. A special damp cupboard may be necessary if a number of objects need to be kept in this state.

Pug mill
When large quantities of clay are needed a pug mill is used to 'mince' the clay and obtain a mixture of an even consistency. Such clay may not need wedging but will require kneading before use.

Tools
Very few special tools are needed. A basic list should include a kitchen rolling-pin and wooden spoon together with the following specialist items: rubber kidneys, for shaping; boxwood modelling tools; slip trailers; wire loop modelling tools; a wire cutter, turning tools. Special pottery tools can be obtained from several firms including Clayglaze and Wengers.

Display design

Display designers are employed by all the major departmental and chain stores to design and make the window and interior displays which promote the sale of goods. Different seasons of the year, such as Christmas and Easter, need special displays and other promotions may require lavish transformations of the interior of large stores. The nature of this work often requires much of the actual fitting of new displays to take place when the stores are closed for normal trading. Some firms employ designers who are permanently based in the stores, while others employ travelling designers who move from town to town changing displays. Display designers require creative abilities in both two- and three-dimensional design, lettering and typography and a knowledge of printing processes. A developed sense of colour and texture, together with drawing skills, are important. There are a number of DATEC courses available in this area of design.

Film and television design

Many of the skills required by film and television companies are those which are equally applicable to other design areas such as graphic design, interior design, stage design and theatre costume design. There are some specialist courses which specialise in training for film and television design.

Basically the television design team usually consists of a designer and a design assistant. The usual route for entry to posts in the BBC is by appointment as a design assistant. Promotion to designer is normally by internal appointment. Design assistants should have training in architectural or exhibition draughtsmanship and must normally have successfully completed a suitable advanced course in an art and design college. The BBC does not run any training courses. Holiday relief design assistants are sometimes appointed from students who have successfully completed a BA or equivalent level course in such areas as interior design, theatre design or architecture, but can also include those who have trained as painters, sculptors, print-makers and industrial and furniture designers.

Furniture design

There are basically two types of furniture designer. There are those who both design and make individual items of furniture and usually work for themselves or in small companies, and those who only design for the mass-production market. Sometimes, however, there is some overlap between these two categories. The designer who makes individual pieces of furniture has to have very high standards of creativity and craftsmanship as the marketing of the product relies on the personal reputation of the designer and on the uniqueness and appropriateness of the finished item. Mass-production designers are often designing for a specific market and work as either free-lance designers for several firms or as an employee of a major manufacturing company. Aesthetics, ergonomics* and a knowledge of the characteristics and capabilities of a wide range of materials, together with high standards of numeracy and draughtsmanship, are necessary. The traditional furniture industry is usually conservative in its attitude to design, and new ideas are often slow to appear in the mass market. The most important developments have been in the use of new materials and new production techniques using advanced technology. Some designers specialise in the conservation and restoration of antique furniture, working for specialist dealers, museums or national institutions.

Glass design

Courses that specialise in glass design sometimes combine the study with ceramics, such as at the City of Birmingham Polytechnic, Buckinghamshire College of Higher Education, North-East Wales Institute of Higher Education and Stourbridge College of Technology and Art. At Leicester Polytechnic, glass can be studied with ceramics and silver and Edinburgh College of Art offers a specialised glass course. The Royal College of Art provides both two- and three-year postgraduate courses, combined with ceramics, leading to the award of M.Des. (RCA).

Interior design

Interior designers tend to work as free-lance designers for private clients or in design partnerships under contract to large public companies, such as restaurant and hotel chains and breweries, where they are responsible for the total look of the interior of buildings. Exhibition design is often part of the job of the interior designer. It is sometimes difficult to establish a successful career as it is nearly always necessary to work with architects who often wish to be responsible for the interior of buildings they have designed. However, the largest architectural practices often employ interior designers as part of their design teams, and the ability to work with other specialists such as structural, heating, ventilating and electrical engineers, together with architects and graphic designers, is most important. A high developed sense of period and style, colour and texture, together with numeracy, draughtsmanship and drawing skills, are all necessary for the professional interior designer.

An interior designer can be required to specify all the requirements for an interior, ranging from small items such as door handles and light switches to carpets, curtains, furniture, wall and ceiling surfaces, kitchens, bathrooms and toilet equipment and the choice of cutlery, china and glass.

Industrial design (engineering)

Industrial designers work in the electronics, plastics, engineering and allied industries, in the automotive and aerospace industries or in design practices serving these industries. The work has close associations with engineering design, ergonomics, aesthetics and design history, and workshop studies form a part of the professional education and training. The range of manufactured items designed by industrial designers is very wide and includes land, air and water transport of all kinds and consumer products, including all the major household items such as refrigerators, cookers, television sets, vacuum cleaners, hi-fi systems, radios and videotape recorders. Also included are the specialised machine tools and other apparatus used for the manufacture of these and other items. A science/design-based general education to GCE 'A' level standard is the normal minimum entry requirement with possible emphasis on mathematics and physics. The Central School of Art and Design, London, offers a three-year First Degree Course leading to the award of BA Honours, and similar courses are available at Leicester Polytechnic, Leeds Polytechnic, Manchester Polytechnic, Napier College, Sheffield City Polytechnic and Teesside Polytechnic. Coventry (Lanchester) Polytechnic offers the only First Degree Industrial Design Transportation Course in the United Kingdom. The Royal College of Art offers postgraduate courses in industrial design.

Jewellery and silversmithing design

One of the most distinctive features of this area of design is that many designers make up their designs themselves rather than have the work done by craftsmen. Their response to materials is therefore a very practical one and a thorough knowledge of the processes is essential for the professional designer.

Jewellers must have an inherent ability to work on a small, three-dimensional scale with particular reference to the decoration of the human form.

There are basically two types of jeweller:
1. The designer/maker, who works in precious metals such as gold, silver and platinum and also in precious stones. Much of this work is traditional in design and is usually purchased either as an investment or as an outward show of wealth. Traditionally, the jewellery trade is divided into 'mount-makers', who design and construct the whole piece but do not work with stones, and 'setters' who cut, shape and finally set the precious stones in the mount.

Precious jewellery is only produced in very small quantities and is often made as a single and unique piece.

2. Designer/maker – costume and fashion jewellery. The designers use materials such as plastics, resins, titanium, silver, brass, copper, wood and ceramics, either singly or in combinations, to produce relatively inexpensive items determined by the demands of the market which is closely related to the influence of fashion. By using machine production methods the unit cost can be very low and good distribution can often ensure large numbers of items being sold in the shops.

The designers who work in either of these two categories can be self-employed and responsible for the making of a complete piece, or they can work in association with specialist firms who may take over the responsibility for one or more parts of the construction process such as casting. The designers who work in precious metals often sell their work direct to their clients and sometimes work to a particular client's commission. Costume and fashion jewellery designers, however, sometimes sell the prototype design to a manufacturer/retailer who is then responsible for the mass-production and marketing. Alternatively, a designer may undertake to get a large order from a retailer mass-produced.

Employment opportunities for makers of precious jewellery are very limited, but jobs sometimes occur at the major firms. The manufacturing jewellers are traditionally specialised into five main areas of work with the firms providing both a service for the designer/craftsman and producing for the mass market. The areas of work are: casting; engraving; polishing/cleaning/barrelling; stone setting; enamelling.

Workshop treatments

Heat.   Jewellers usually require heat to soften or 'anneal' the metal to make it more pliable and to 'silver solder' to join metals. The most usual method for obtaining the necessary heat is to use a mixture of gas and air, provided by a compressor, blowpipe or bellows.

Cleaning.   After the annealing or soldering process the metal must be cleaned by submerging it in a solution of acid and water, a process known as 'pickling'. Different metals require different acid solutions for this process. When the metal appears pale and clean it is washed and scrubbed with pumice powder, rinsed and dried. The construction of a piece of jewellery involves several different types of tools:

1. Cutting – saws, drills, files.
2. Shaping and forming – raising, bending, planishing, rolling, wire drawing.
3. Joining – soldering, riveting.

Silversmithing

This is a separate design area, allied to jewellery in that the main materials used are metals but not necessarily silver. Much of the work is closely related to product design, and new materials such as stainless steel have revolutionised the traditional hand processes. Cutlery, once an important area, is now nearly all mass-produced and the substitution of plastics and wood for handles is an example of the changes that have been brought about due to the high cost of labour and the increased cost of materials. The market for traditional silversmithing, such as trophy-making, is very small.

Courses

There are a number of degree courses available in both jewellery and silversmithing, including courses at the City of Birmingham Polytechnic, City of London Polytechnic, Loughborough College of Art and Design and Sheffield City Polytechnic. Middlesex Polytechnic offers a four-year sandwich course in jewellery and ceramics.

Model-making

Industrial model-makers work on architectural, theatre, film, television, industrial and product models, working with a wide range of materials including wood, metals, plastics and a variety of adhesives. The ability to work accurately on a very small scale, together with both machine and hand craft skills, is required. Model-makers creatively interpret and construct three-dimensional models from two-dimensional drawings. The Medway College of Design at Rochester in Kent has a well-established course in industrial model-making at Higher Diploma level.

Product design

The term 'product design' can be misleading. In relation to art and design it nearly always refers to the surface design or styling of a product. Such designers may work with engineering designers, interior designers and architects in the designing or modification of consumer products, electrical and mechanical machinery, transport systems, telecommunications systems and architecture. There are specific courses in product design, and several of the multidisciplinary three-dimensional courses can lead to work in this area. The Polytechnic of the South Bank in London offers a four-year sandwich course in engineering product design and some engineering designers are themselves qualified product designers, having first obtained an engineering qualification and then specialised in product design at postgraduate level. A knowledge of production methods, aesthetics and ergonomics and the ability to design creatively for a wide range of materials including wood, metals and plastics are essential. A high degree of numeracy and the ability to work with a team of specialists in other disciplines are also important.

Stage design

The number of career opportunities for designers who wish to specialise in this area is very limited and the training opportunities are similarly restricted. Designing for the stage is basically a three-dimensional exercise and includes not only work for the theatre but for opera, ballet, films, television, experimental theatre and community arts projects. Any production, however small, usually involves a team of specialists working under the guidance of a director and can include lighting experts, costume designers, set dressers, make-up experts and the supporting craftsmen such as carpenters and electricians. A creative imagination is essential, combined with a highly developed sense of colour and attention to detail. A knowledge of historical styles and periods and the ability to direct a team of experts is also necessary. Stage designers combine many of the talents of architects, interior designers, display designers and fashion designers.

Visual effects designers

The BBC Visual Effects Department recruits all its design staff from visual effects design assistants already employed within the department. The design assistants construct and operate all types of effects, working in such materials as metals, plastics and wood. Workshop experience, including the operation of machine tools, is required and a thorough understanding of the fundamentals of physics, electricity and chemistry is essential. Students with a background of sculpture, painting, model-making, pyrotechnics and optics, together with the ability to produce good representational drawings and with previous experience in this area of work, are at an advantage. The work can be physically arduous and good health is also required.

2.6 FINE ART

Fine art courses offer an excellent, broad, liberal education in the visual arts. They are, in general, not primarily concerned with the training of potential painters and sculptors, although a very small number of graduates will earn their living in this way. They do, however, provide young people with a unique education and training of the visual senses, and the attitudes and concepts which are learned provide a view of the world and all its activities which are life enhancing and marketable.

Students who are determined to succeed as professional fine artists will probably do so. The State offers no support once the student has left college and this is understandable. Any bureaucracy tends to work towards the *status quo*, and once a fine artist is prepared to compromise in order to survive it is difficult to maintain any integrity. Teaching offers some financial support by the provision of part-time contracts in art and design schools and colleges, but this traditional area of employment is changing due to both economic and demographic changes.

For the minority who have the talent and motivation to succeed as professional artists the support of professional colleagues and friends is often essential. There are no 'rules' or established criteria and this can make the experience both stimulating and isolating. In the early stages the degree of permanence of any work is unimportant. Dissatisfaction with systems of sponsorship such as that of the Arts Council of Great Britain or the influence of commercial dealers through the gallery networks has led many fine artists to explore ways of producing work which is not obviously marketable and in so doing they have changed the nature of the work itself. Nevertheless, the dealers have also adapted to these changes and have encompassed in some form or other many of the art forms that were thought to be impossible to market. Traditional activities such as painting and sculpture periodically recharge themselves, but many fine artists now find their best means of expression through photography, video, film, theatre and community arts. Social and economic changes affect young artists like everyone else and their work merely reflects the world in which we all live. It is important not to have a fixed idea of what is art. This can limit individual creative responses to changing situations.

Scenic artists. Film television

Artists responsible for the painting of backcloths, gauzes and decorative features such as floor designs are known as scenic artists. Such work can also include the representation of carpets, curtains and tapestries and special tasks associated with a particular historical period or style. Art and design school training to diploma level is normally required and the major television companies prefer artists with some previous direct experience of work in theatre, film or television. The number of career opportunities is very limited.

2.7 CONSERVATION

The conservation and restoration of works of art, buildings, furniture, books and documents require particular skills and a knowledge of the history of art, design, architecture and archaeology. Museums and major art galleries probably provide the largest number of career opportunities, but the number of posts are very limited. Specialist courses, such as the Courtauld Institute of Art Diploma in the Conservation of Paintings course or the Paper Conservation course at Camberwell School of Art, provide for professional education and training. The museum services, National Trust, Department of the Environment and other agencies who are responsible for the maintenance and conservation of works of art of all kinds sometimes have specialised departments dealing with this work. Much conservation work is scientifically based and a knowledge of physics and chemistry is often essential for some courses.

2.8 ART AND DESIGN HISTORY

There are a number of career opportunities available for art and design historians as journalists, academics, teachers, museum and gallery staff, conservationists and restorers. The Courtauld Institute of Art specialises in the study of art history and is one of the Senate Institutes of the University of London. It offers courses leading to the award of degree in the history of European Art and applications should be made through UCCA. Degree courses in the history of art are also available at a number of other universities, including Bristol, where it can be combined with the study of a modern language; Cambridge; East Anglia, where it can be combined with the study of literature; and Reading, where it can be combined with the study of art. There are courses in the history of design leading to the award of CNAA degrees at Brighton and Manchester Polytechnics and a course in the history of art and design in the modern period is available at Leicester Polytechnic. The history of modern art, design and film can be studied for a first degree at Newcastle upon Tyne Polytechnic and the history of art, design and film at Sheffield City Polytechnic. The North Staffordshire Polytechnic offers a degree course in the history of design and the visual arts. There is a growing interest in the history of design, and the development of DATEC design courses may provide some opportunities for design historians to work alongside practising designers and designers in training. The Boilerhouse Project at the Victoria and Albert Museum and the work of the Design Councils further strengthens this important aspect of design education.

CHAPTER 3

Visual research

Fig. 3.1   Visual research – DATEC General Art and Design Course students from Barnet College on a Field Study Course at Kilve Court, Somerset

3.1   EDUCATIONAL VISITS

Visits to art galleries, museums and other centres are an important part of the work of many artists and designers. This will often involve travel and a knowledge of sources for research material is, therefore, invaluable.

Discovering a small, specialist museum can be very rewarding and most towns have a local museum with curators who are usually very familiar with their area. Major museums often provide special research facilities for students, including study rooms. Explore local possibilities. Churches are a rich source for study, particularly for stained glass and carvings. Local cemeteries are a good source for the study of lettering. Many local authorities have parks departments who maintain large greenhouses for growing plants for public spaces: they are often willing to let students work in the greenhouses studying tropical and semi-tropical plants. College and public libraries are another source of research material. The UK national inter-library lending system is the best in the world and it is possible to obtain almost any book from any source. The British Library has a newspaper and periodical library located in North London. Some public libraries have specialist departments and it is always worth consulting the staff about particular interests. There are some useful publications which can be of help. The guide *Museums and Galleries in Great Britain and Ireland* published annually (ABC Historic Publications) is an inexpensive and useful reference guide to over 1,000 centres. The National Trust publish a guide and map to their houses and gardens which are open to the public. The annual *Historic Houses, Castles and Gardens* guide (ABC Historic Publications) lists the majority of privately owned houses open to the public.

If a visit to a National Trust property or a private house is planned, particularly during the summer months, always telephone beforehand and check that making sketches or taking photographs is allowed. It is also worth checking on research facilities for students when visiting museums and galleries. There are strict rules about taking photographs in some museums. Information on ancient monuments and historic buildings which are the responsibility of the Department of the Environment can be obtained from a series of guides published by Her Majesty's Stationery Office.

It is impossible to list all the sources for research. This section of the book identifies some areas which have proved useful. Using one source as a starting-point can lead to the discovery of other, more personal, sources.

Equipment

Some basic equipment is needed. Keep this to a minimum. If an important section of a museum is cluttered up with students and their equipment it makes worthwhile study almost impossible. A camera with a flash is invaluable. Remember to obtain permission before taking photographs indoors. A sketch-book, rather than a sketch-pad, together with a range of drawing materials, inks, a small, leakproof container of water, erasers and a knife for sharpening, should complete a basic kit. All these items can be comfortably carried in a designer's box. Avoid taking a drawing board, but a small, collapsible, stool would be a bonus.

3.2 STUDENT TRAVEL

British Rail

Railcard – Half-price train travel

The British Rail railcard, for which a charge is made, entitles students or anyone under the age of twenty-four to half-price travel on second class ordinary single or return Awayday (day/day off-peak return) tickets. There are special conditions attached to the issue of these tickets. To qualify, applicants must be under twenty-four or in full-time education attending an educational establishment for over fifteen hours weekly and for at least twenty weeks of the full academic year. All applicants must complete a railcard application form and obtain certification of proof of age. Two passport-type photographs are also required. Where railcards are issued at a college campus student travel office a college registration card, bearing a passport-type photograph and valid for the period to be covered by the railcard, is acceptable in place of certification of proof of age.

Inter-rail ticket (European travel)

Maximum age limit twenty-six years. British Rail inter-rail tickets entitle holders to one month's unlimited second-class rail travel in Europe, and half-fare travel in Great Britain. It also covers Sealink ships. Applications should be made at any main-line British Rail station. A valid passport must be produced before the ticket can be issued. The ticket is valid for travel in the following countries: Austria, Belgium, France, Denmark, Finland, Greece, Hungary, Italy, Luxembourg, Morocco, The Netherlands, Norway, Portugal, Roumania, Spain, Sweden, Switzerland, West Germany and Yugoslavia.

Transalpino tickets (British Rail)

Maximum age limit twenty-six years. Transalpino offer a low tariff system known as BIGE. This entitles holders to reduced fares from London and more than 60 provincial stations to over 2000 destinations in Europe. Reductions on standard rail fares vary, but can be as much as 50 per cent. Obtain a British Rail Transalpino leaflet from main stations for full details.

Travel in London

London Transport (buses and Underground) do not offer any special student travel facilities. They do, however, offer concessions to all members of the public.

Cheap day return.   Available for Underground travel from 10.00 a.m. Mondays to Fridays and all day Saturdays and Sundays.

Central Tube Rover.   Unlimited travel for a whole day on any of the Circle Line trains or other lines inside the Circle Line. Also covers Waterloo.

Red Bus Rovers.   Unlimited travel for a whole day on the buses.

Bus flat fares.   Flat fares operate on routes outside the central London area. Available at all times.

Off-peak maximum bus fares.   Available off-peak from Monday to Friday and at week-ends. For travel into and beyond the flat fare area.

Go-as-you-please ticket.   Available for three, four or seven days for all journeys over most of the Underground and on all London Red buses.
For full information on London Transport services telephone 01 222 1234 any time – day or night.

3.3 RESEARCH CENTRES

Ceramics glass

Bedford   Cecil Higgins Art Gallery, Castle Close. Open weekdays (except Mondays) *from* 12.30 p.m. to 5.00 p.m. Tel: 0234 211222

Brighton   Brighton Museum, Church Street. Open Tuesdays to Saturdays 10.00 a.m. to 5.45 p.m. Admission free. Tel: 0273 603005

Cheltenham   Cheltenham Museum, Clarence Street. Open Mondays to Saturdays 10.00 a.m. to 5.30 p.m. Admission free. Tel: 0242 37431

Durham   Gulbenkian Museum of Oriental Art and Archaeology, Elvet Hill. Open Mondays to Fridays 9.30 a.m. to 1.00 p.m. and 2.15 p.m. to 5.00 p.m. Admission charge. Tel: 0385 66711

London   Percival David Foundation of Chinese Art (Chinese Ceramics) 53 Gordon Square, WC1H OPD. Open Mondays 2.00 p.m. to 5.00 p.m., Tuesdays to Fridays 10.30 a.m. to 5.00 p.m. and Saturdays 10.30 a.m. to 1.00 p.m.
The British Museum and the Victoria and Albert Museum have important collections of china and glass. For details of opening times see under Design and Fine art.

Nottingham   Nottingham Castle Museum. Open daily from 10.00
a.m. Admission free. Tel: 0602 41188

St Helens   Pilkington Glass Museum, Prescot Road. Open Mondays
to Fridays 10.00 a.m. to 5.00 p.m., Saturdays and Sundays 2.00 p.m.
to 4.30 p.m. Admission free. Tel: 0744 28882

Stoke-on-Trent   City Museum, Broad Street, Hanley. Open weekdays
10.30 a.m. to 5.00 p.m. Admission free. Tel: 0782 29611
    Gladstone Pottery Museum, Uttoxeter Road, Longton. Open
according to season 10.30 a.m. to 5.30 p.m. Closed Mondays from
October to March. Admission charge. Tel: 0782 319232

See also the Fitzwilliam Museum, Cambridge (Fine Art Section) and
the Ashmolean Museum, Oxford (Fine Art Section). The majority of
national and regional museums have important collections of ceramics
and glass.

Costume

Bath   Museum of Costume, Assembly Rooms. Open – Winter –
Mondays to Saturdays 10.00 a.m. to 5.00 p.m., Sundays 11.00 a.m. to
5.00 p.m. Summer – Mondays to Saturdays 9.30 p.m. to 6.00 p.m.
Admission charge. Tel: 0225 61111

Castle Howard, York   Castle Howard Costume Galleries, Castle
Howard, York. Open daily from Easter to October 11.30 a.m. to 5.00
p.m. Admission charge. Tel: Coneysthorpe 333

Manchester   The Gallery of English Costume, Platt Hall, Platt Fields,
Rusholme. Open weekdays 10 a.m. to 6.00 p.m., Sundays 2.00 p.m. to
6.00 p.m. Closed from November to February. Tel: 061 224 5217

Nottingham   Museum of Costume and Textiles, Castlegate. Open
daily 10.00 a.m. to 5.00 p.m. Admission free. Tel: 0602 411881

See also the Victoria and Albert Museum, which has a major collection
of costumes (see Design section), and the collections of other major
national and regional museums. The museums of the armed services
have collections of military uniforms and the armour collections at the
Tower of London are excellent (see Military section). Costume research
can also be carried out by studying paintings of various periods. The
collections at the Rangers House, Blackheath; Montacute House,
Yeovil, and the National Portrait Gallery (see Fine art) may be
particularly useful.

Crafts (including ethnological collections)

Bath The American Museum in Britain, Claverton Manor, near Bath. Normally open from April to October daily (except Mondays) from 2.00 p.m. to 5.00 p.m. Education Department Tel: 0225 63538

Hull Town Docks Museum, Queen Victoria Square. Open weekdays 10.00 a.m. to 5.00 p.m. Admission free. Tel: 0482 223111

Liverpool Merseyside County Museum, William Brown Street. Open weekdays 10.00 a.m. to 5.00 p.m. Admission free. Tel: 051 207 0001

London Bethnal Green Museum (a branch of the Victoria and Albert Museum). Open Mondays to Thursdays 10.00 a.m. to 6.00 p.m., Saturdays 10.00 a.m. to 6.00 p.m. Sundays 2.30 p.m. to 6.00 p.m. Museum of childhood. Admission free. Tel: 01 980 2415

British Crafts Centre, 43 Earlham Street, WC2. Open Mondays to Fridays 10.00 a.m. to 5.30 p.m. Saturdays 10.00 a.m. to 4.00 p.m. Tel: 01 836 6993

Crafts Council Gallery and Resource Centre, 11/12 Waterloo Place, Lower Regent Street, SW1Y 4AU. Open Tuesdays to Saturdays 10.00 a.m. to 5.00 p.m., Sundays 2.00 p.m. to 5.00 p.m. Admission charge. Tel: 01 930 4811

Fenton House, Hampstead Grove, Hampstead, NW3. Collection of early musical instruments. Open Wednesdays to Sundays 2.00 p.m. to 6.00 p.m. Admission charge. Tel: 01 435 3471

Horniman Museum, London Road, Forest Hill, SE23 3PQ. Open Mondays to Saturdays 10.30 a.m. to 6.00 p.m. Admission free. Tel: 01 699 2339

Museum of Mankind, 6, Burlington Gardens, W1X 2EX (Ethnological Collection of the British Museum). Open weekdays 10.00 a.m. to 5.00 p.m., Sundays 2.30 p.m. to 6.00 p.m. Admission free. Tel: 01 437 2224

Northleach, Gloucestershire Cotswold Countryside Collection, Fosseway. Open during the summer months. Weekdays 10.00 a.m. to 6.00 p.m., Sundays 2.00 p.m. to 6.00 p.m. Admission charge. Tel: 0285 5611

Oxford Pitt-Rivers Museum, Parkes Road. Open Mondays to Saturdays 2.00 p.m. to 4.00 p.m. Admission free. Tel: 0865 54979

Reading Museum of English Rural Life (University of Reading),

Fig. 3.2   *Museum of English Rural Life – Reading, Domestic Section*

Whiteknights Reading (Fig. 3.2). Open Tuesdays to Fridays
10.00 a.m. to 4.30 p.m. Saturdays 10.00 a.m. to 1.00 p.m. and
2.00 p.m. to 4.30 p.m. Admission free. Permanent exhibition of
agricultural tools and implements, rural industries and domestic
equipment, together with a collection of farm wagons and ploughs. The
photographic library contains more than 250,000 prints and negatives
from the mid-nineteenth century to the present day. Tel: 0734 85123

St Fagans, South Glamorgan Wales   Welsh Folk Museum, St
Fagans Castle. Open weekdays 10.00 a.m. to 5.00 p.m., Sundays 2.30
p.m. to 5.00 p.m. Admission charge. Tel: 0222 569441

Stocksfield, Northumberland (14 miles west of Newcastle)   National
Tractor and Farm Museum, Newton near Stocksfield. Open daily 10.00
a.m. to 6.00 p.m. Admission charge. Museum of the Year 1981. Major
exhibition of farm tractors, farming bygones, static engines and farm
trades. Also known as the Hunday Museum. Tel: Stocksfield 2553

York   York Castle Museum, Tower Street. Open according to season.
Mondays to Saturdays from 9.30 a.m. Sundays from 10.00 a.m.
Admission charge. Tel: 0904 53611

Design

Bramber nr Steyning, West Sussex   The National Butterfly Museum, St Mary's. Major display of butterflies and moths housed in beautiful historic house. Photo-library with more than 10,000 transparencies and prints. Library with 2000 volumes and research facilities. Open every day (except 25/26 December) 10.00 a.m. to 5.00 p.m. Admission charge. Tel: 0903 813158

Brighton   The Royal Pavilion, Regency Palace and Exhibition. Open daily 10.00 a.m. to 5.00 p.m. (late opening to 7.30 p.m. during July, August and September). Admission charge. Tel: 0273 603005

London   Clockmakers' Company Museum, Guildhall Library, Aldermanbury Street, EC2P 2EJ. Open Mondays to Fridays 9.30 a.m. to 5.00 p.m. Admission free. Tel: 01 606 3030

The Design Centre, 28 Haymarket, SW1. Continually changing display of British-made goods. Reference section and excellent design bookshop. Open Mondays to Saturdays 9.00 a.m. to 8.00 p.m. Admission free. Tel: 01 839 8000

Goldsmiths' Hall, Foster Lane, Cheapside, EC2. The collection of the Goldsmiths' Company. Tel: 01 606 8971 for special permission to study the collection.

Geffrye Museum, Kingsland Road, Shoreditch, E2 8EA Exhibition of period rooms from about 1600. Excellent examples of furniture. Open Tuesdays to Saturdays 10.00 a.m. to 5.00 p.m., Sundays 2.00 p.m. to 5.00 p.m. Admission free. Tel: 01 739 8368

Leighton House, 12 Holland Park Road, Kensington, W14. A good example of High Victorian interior design. Open daily 11.00 a.m. to 5.00 p.m. Tel: 01 602 3316

National Film Archive, 81 Dean Street, W1. Open 10.00 a.m. to 6.00 p.m. Tel: 01 437 4355 for appointment. Not open to the general public.

National Postal Museum, King Edward Building, King Edward Street, EC1. Major display of postage stamps. Photograph service. Research facilities. Library. Open Mondays to Fridays 10.00 a.m. to 4.30 p.m. Tel: 01 432 3851

Pollocks' Toy Museum, 1 Scala Street, W1P 1LT Open Mondays to Saturdays 10.00 a.m. to 5.00 p.m. Admission charge. Tel: 01 636 3452

Royal Botanic Gardens (Kew Gardens). Open according to season from 10.00 a.m. Admission charge.

Science Museum, Exhibition Road, South Kensington. Open weekdays 10.00 a.m. to 6.00 p.m., Sundays 2.30 p.m. to 6.00 p.m. Admission free. Tel: 01 589 3456

Victoria and Albert Museum, Cromwell Road, South Kensington, SW7. Open Mondays to Thursdays and Saturdays 10.00 a.m. to 5.50 p.m., Sundays 2.30 p.m. to 5.50 p.m. Admission charge. Tel: 01 589 6371

William Morris Gallery, Water House, Lloyd Park, Forest Road, Walthamstow, E17. Open weekdays 10.00 a.m. to 5.00 p.m. Tel: 01 527 5544

Manchester   National Paper Museum, 97 Grosvenor Street. Open Mondays to Saturdays 10.00 a.m. to 5.00 p.m. Admission free. Tel: 061 273 6636

Northampton   Central Museum Footwear Exhibition, Guildhall Road. Open Mondays to Saturdays 10.00 a.m. to 6.00 p.m. Admission free. Tel: 0604 34881

Rothbury, Northumberland   Cragside, near Rothbury. House modified by the architect Norman Shaw and containing excellent examples of Victorian interiors. Open daily during the summer months 1.00 p.m. to 6.00 p.m. Closed on Mondays. Admission charge.

Street, Somerset   Street Shoe Museum (C. & C. Clark Ltd) High Street. Open (by appointment) to students for study all the year. Open to the public from May to October. A large and comprehensive collection of shoes and related items from Roman and through medieval times to the present day. The collection includes costume illustrations, fashion plates and cartoons from the eighteenth century onwards. Admission free. Tel: 0458 43131

The majority of national and regional museums have substantial collections of items which can provide excellent reference material for the study of all aspects of design.

Fine arts

This section includes public galleries and museums that have both permanent collections and temporary exhibitions on display and commercial or grant-aided galleries that regularly exhibit contemporary work. Details of current exhibitions can be obtained from the national and local press as well as from specialist art and design magazines. Galleries that have changing exhibitions are marked with an asterisk*.

Belfast   Octagon Gallery,* 1 Lower Crescent.

Ulster Museum, Botanic Gardens, Belfast, BT9 5AB. Open weekdays 10.00 a.m. to 5.00 p.m., Sundays 2.30 p.m. to 5.30 p.m. Admission free. Tel: 0232 668251

Fig. 3.3 (a) *Museum Study at British Museum by DATEC General Art and Design Course students – Barnet College*
(b) *Museum Study of Ceramics of DATEC General Art and Design Course students – Barnet College*

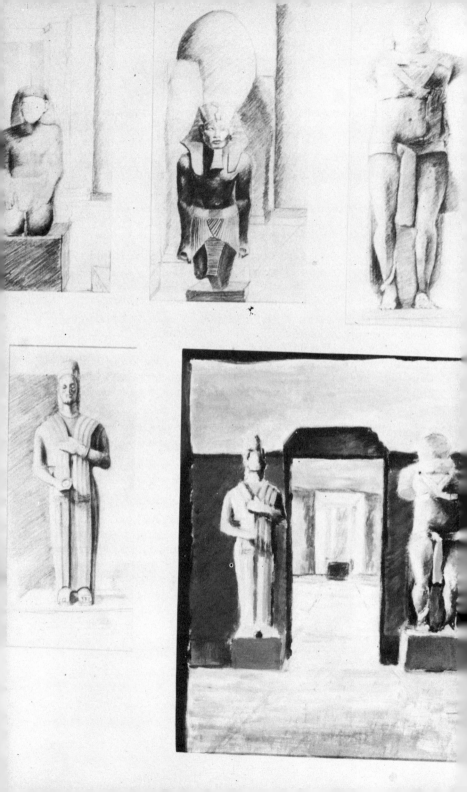

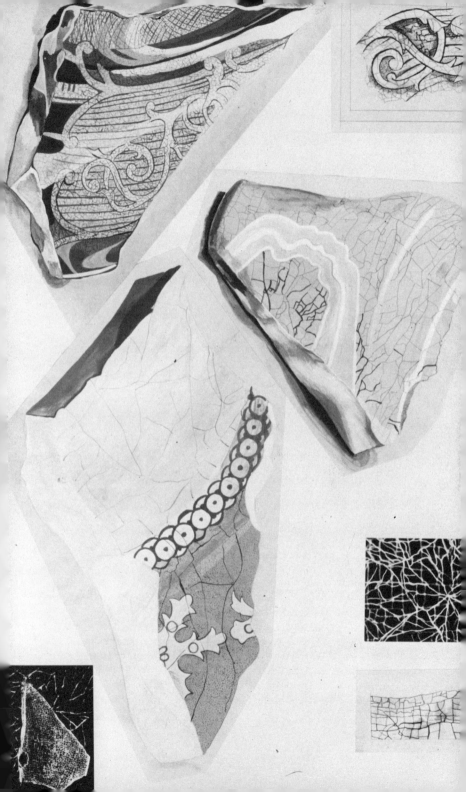

Birmingham   Museum and Art Gallery, Chamberlain Square, Birmingham, B3 3DH Open Mondays to Saturdays 10.00 a.m. to 5.30 p.m. Sundays 2.00 p.m. to 5.30 p.m. Admission free. Tel: 021 235 2834. Education Department Tel: 021 235 3890

Ikon Gallery,★ John Bright Street.

Bournemouth   Russell-Cotes Art Gallery, East Cliff.

Bradford   Art Gallery and Museum, Cartwright Hall, Open Tuesdays to Saturdays 10.00 a.m. to 5.00 p.m. Admission free. Tel: 0274 493313

Brighton   Axis Gallery,★ 12 Market Street, The Lanes.

Burstow Gallery, Brighton College,★ Eastern Road.

Barclaycraft Gallery,★ 7, East Street. Gardner Centre Gallery,★ University of Sussex.

Bristol   Arnolfini Art Centre,★ Narrow Quay, Bristol, BS1 4QA. Tel: 0272 299191

Cambridge   Fitzwilliam Museum, Trumpington Street. Open Tuesdays to Saturdays. Lower Galleries, Ceramics, etc. 10.00 a.m. to 2.00 p.m. Upper Galleries, Fine Art, 2.00 p.m. to 5.00 p.m. Admission free. Tel: 0223 69501/3

Kettles Yard Gallery,★ Northampton Street. Open daily 12.30 p.m. to 5.30 p.m., Sundays 2.00 p.m. to 5.30 p.m. Tel: 0223 352124

Cardiff   National Museum of Wales. Open Weekdays 10.00 a.m. to 5.00 p.m., Sundays 2.30 p.m. to 5.00 p.m. Tel: 0222 397951

Colchester   Minories Gallery,★ 74 High Street.

Dublin   National Gallery of Ireland, Merrion Square. Open weekdays 10.00 a.m. to 6.00 p.m., Sundays 2.00 p.m. to 5.00 p.m. Tel: Dublin 767571

Hugh Lane Gallery of Modern Art, Charlement House, Parnell Square. Open weekdays Tuesdays to Saturdays 9.30 a.m. to 6.00 p.m. Sundays 11.00 a.m. to 2.00 p.m. Tel: Dublin 741903

Durham   Bowes Museum, Barnard Castle. Open Mondays to Saturdays according to season from 10.00 a.m., Sundays from 2.00 p.m. Admission charge. Tel: 0833 37139

Eastbourne   Tower Art Gallery,★ Borough Lane.

Edinburgh   City Art Centre,* 1–4 Market Street. Open weekdays 10.00 a.m. to 5.00 p.m. Admission free. Tel: 031 225 1131

Fruit Market Gallery,* 29 Market Street. Open weekdays 10.00 a.m. to 5.30 p.m. Tel: 031 226 5781

National Gallery of Scotland, The Mound, Edinburgh, EH2 2EL. Open weekdays 10.00 a.m. to 5.00 p.m., Sundays 2.00 p.m. to 5.00 p.m. Admission free. Tel: 031 556 8921

Royal Scottish Museum, Chambers Street, Edinburgh, EH1 1JF, Open weekdays 10.00 a.m. to 5.00 p.m., Sundays 2.00 p.m. to 5.00 p.m. Admission free. Tel: 031 225 7534

Scottish National Gallery of Modern Art, Royal Botanic Gardens, Edinburgh, EH3 5LP. Open weekdays 10.00 a.m. to 6.00 p.m. Sundays 2.00 p.m. to 6.00 p.m. Admission free. Tel: 031 332 3754

Scottish National Portrait Gallery, Queen Street, EH2 1JD. Open weekdays 10.00 a.m. to 5.00 p.m., Sundays 2.00 p.m. to 5.00 p.m. Admission free. Tel: 031 556 8921

Glasgow   Art Gallery and Museum, Kelvingrove. Open weekdays 10.00 a.m. to 5.00 p.m., Sundays 2.00 p.m. to 5.00 p.m. Admission free. Tel: 041 334 1134

Burrell Collection. Tel: 041 632 1350

Hunterian Collection Art Gallery, University of Glasgow Hillhead street. Open Mondays to Fridays 10.00 a.m. to 5.00 a.m. Saturdays 9.30 a.m. to 1.00 p.m. Tel: 041 339 8855

Hull   Ferens Art Gallery, Queen Victoria Square. Open weekdays 10.00 a.m. to 5.00 p.m. Admission free. Tel: 0482 223111

Leeds   Leeds City Art Gallery. Open weekdays 10.00 a.m. to 6.00 p.m. Sundays 2.00 p.m. to 5.00 p.m. Admission free. Tel: 0532 462495

Leicester   Leicestershire Museum and Art Gallery, New Walk. Open weekdays 10.00 a.m. to 5.30 p.m. Admission free. Tel: 0533 554100

Liverpool   Open Eye Gallery,* 90–92 Whitechapel.

Walker Art Gallery, William Brown Street. Open weekdays 10.00 a.m. to 5.00 p.m. Tel: 051 227 5234 (see also Crafts section)

London   Acme Gallery,* 43 Shelton Street, Covent Garden, WC2. Open Mondays to Saturdays 11.00 a.m. to 6.00 p.m. Tel: 01 240 4047

Fig. 3.4   Visual research study – Foundation Course student – Barnet College

Air Gallery,* 6/8 Rosebery Avenue, EC1. Open Mondays to Fridays 11.00 a.m. to 6.00 p.m., Saturdays 11.00 a.m. to 2.00 p.m. Tel: 01 287 7751

Angela Flowers Gallery,* 11 Tottenham Mews, W1. Open Mondays to Fridays 10.30 a.m. to 5.30 p.m., Saturdays 10.30 a.m. to 12.30 p.m. Tel: 01 637 3089

Blond Fine Art,* 33 Sackville Street, W.1. Open Mondays to Fridays 10.00 a.m. to 6.00 p.m., Saturdays 10.00 a.m. to 1.00 p.m. Tel: 01 437 1230

British Museum, Great Russell Street, W.1. Open weekdays 10.00 a.m. to 5.00 p.m., Sundays 2.30 p.m. to 6.00 p.m. Admission free. Tel: 01 636 1555

Browse & Darby,* 19 Cork Street, W.1. Open Mondays to Fridays 10.00 a.m. to 5.30 p.m. Tel: 01 734 7984

Buckingham Palace – The Queen's Gallery, Buckingham Palace Road, S.W.1. Open Tuesdays to Saturdays, 11.00 a.m. to 5.00 p.m., Sundays 2.00 p.m. to 5.00 p.m. Admission charge.

Camden Arts Centre,* Arkwright Road, Finchley Road, NW3. Open Mondays to Saturdays 11.00 a.m. to 6.00 p.m. Tel: 01 435 2643

Christopher Wood Gallery,* 15 Motcomb Street, SW1. Open Mondays to Fridays 9.30 a.m. to 5.30 p.m. Tel: 01 235 9141

Courtauld Institute Galleries, Woburn Square, W1. Open weekdays 10.00 a.m. to 5.00 p.m., Sundays 2.00 p.m. to 5.00 p.m. Admission charge. Tel: 01 580 1015

Crane Arts,* 321 Kings Road, SW3. Open Mondays to Saturdays, 10.00 a.m. to 6.00 p.m. Tel: 01 352 5857

Curwen Gallery,* 1 Colville Place, Whitfield Street, W.1. Tel: 01 636 1459

Drian Gallery,* 7 Porchester Place, W2. Open Mondays to Fridays, 10.00 a.m. to 5.00 p.m., Saturdays 10.00 a.m. to 1.00 p.m. Tel: 01 723 9473

Dulwich Picture Gallery, College Road, SE21. Open Tuesdays to Saturdays 10.00 a.m. to 5.00 p.m., Sundays 2.00 p.m. to 5.00 p.m. Admission free. Tel: 01 693 5254

Fischer Fine Art,* 30 King Street, St James's, SW1. Open Mondays to Fridays 10.00 a.m. to 5.30 p.m. Saturdays 10.00 a.m. to 12:30 p.m. Tel: 01 839 3942

Gimpel Fils,* 30 Davies Street, W1. Open Mondays to Fridays 9.30 a.m. to 5.30 p.m., Saturdays 10.00 a.m. to 1.00 p.m. Tel: 01 493 2488

Goethe Institute,* 50 Princes Gate, Exhibition Road, SW7. Tel: 01 581 3344

Hayward Gallery, Belvedere Road, South Bank, SE1. For details of temporary exhibitions see national press or telephone 01 928 3144

House Gallery,* 62 Regent's Park Road, NW1. Open Tuesdays to Sundays 11.00 a.m. to 6.00 p.m. Tel: 01 586 5170

Institute of Contemporary Arts (ICA),* Nash House, The Mall, SW1. For details of temporary exhibitions and theatre/film programmes telephone 01 930 0493. Theatre box office Tel: 01 930 3647

Iveagh Bequest, Kenwood, Hampstead Lane, NW3. Open daily 10.00 a.m. to 5.00 p.m. Admission free. Tel: 01 348 1286

Juda Rowan Gallery,* 31a Bruton Place, Berkeley Square and 11 Tottenham Mews, off Tottenham Street, W1. Open daily from 10.00 a.m. to 6.00 p.m., Saturdays 10.00 a.m. to 1.00 p.m. Bruton Street, Tel: 01 493 3727; Tottenham Mews, Tel: 01 637 5517

Knoedler Gallery,* 22 Cork Street, W1. Open Mondays to Fridays 10.00 a.m. to 5.00 p.m., Saturdays 10.00 a.m. to 1.00 p.m. Tel: 01 493 1572

Lefevre Gallery,* 30 Bruton Street, W1. Open Mondays to Fridays 10.00 a.m. to 5.00 p.m., Saturdays 10.00 a.m. to 1.00 p.m. Tel: 01 493 1572

Lisson Gallery,* first floor, 56 Whitfield Street, W1. Open Mondays to Fridays 10.00 a.m. to 6.00 p.m., Saturdays 10.00 a.m. to 1.00 p.m. Tel: 01 631 0942

Lumley Cazalet Gallery,* 24 Davies Street, W1. Open Mondays to Fridays 10.00 a.m. to 6.00 p.m. Tel: 01 499 5058

Marlborough Fine Art,* 6 Albemarle Street, W1. Open Mondays to Fridays 10.00 a.m. to 6.00 p.m., Saturdays 10.00 a.m. to 12.30 p.m. Tel: 01 629 5161

Mayor Gallery,* 22a Cork Street, W1. Open Mondays to Fridays 10.00 a.m. to 5.30 p.m., Saturdays 10.00 a.m. to 1.00 p.m. Tel: 01 734 3558

Mercury Gallery,* 28 Cork Street, W1. Open Mondays to Fridays 10.00 a.m. to 5.30 p.m., Saturdays 10.00 a.m. to 12.30 p.m. Tel: 01 734 7800

National Gallery, Trafalgar Square, WC2. Open weekdays 10.00 a.m. to 6.00 p.m., Sundays 2.00 p.m. to 6.00 p.m. Admission free. Tel: 01 839 3321

National Portrait Gallery, St Martin's Place, Trafalgar Square, WC2. Open Mondays to Fridays 10.00 a.m. to 5.00 p.m., Saturdays

10.00 a.m. to 6.00 p.m., Sundays 2.00 p.m. to 6.00 p.m. Admission free. Tel: 01 930 1552

New Art Centre,* 41 Sloane Street, SW1. Open Mondays to Fridays 10.00 a.m. to 6.00 p.m. Saturdays 10.00 a.m. to 1.00 p.m. Tel: 01 235 5844

Nicholas Treadwell Gallery,* 38 Chiltern Street, W1. Open Mondays to Fridays 10.00 a.m. to 6.00 p.m., Saturdays 10.00 a.m. to 1.00 p.m. Tel: 01 486 1414

Nigel Greenwood Gallery,* 41 Sloane Gardens, SW1. Open Mondays to Fridays. Tel: 01 730 8824

Piccadilly Gallery,* 16 Cork Street, W1. Open Mondays to Fridays 10.00 a.m. to 5.30 p.m. Tel: 01 629 2875

Rangers House, Chesterfield Walk, Blackheath, SE10. Open daily 10.00 a.m. to 5.00 p.m. (winter months 10.00 a.m. to 4.00 p.m.) Admission free. Tel: 01 853 0035

Redfern Gallery,* 20 Cork Street, W1. Open daily Mondays to Fridays 10.00 a.m. to 5.30 p.m. Tel: 01 734 1732

Royal Academy of Arts, Piccadilly, W1. Loan exhibitions throughout the year. Open daily 10.00 a.m. to 6.00 p.m. For details see national press or telephone 01 734 9052

Serpentine Gallery, Kensington Gardens, W2. Temporary exhibitions of contemporary art. Opening times vary according to the season starting at 10.00 a.m. each weekday. Admission free. For details see national press or telephone 01 402 6075

Sir John Soane's Museum, 13 Lincoln's Inn Fields, WC2. Open Tuesdays to Saturdays, 10.00 a.m. to 5.00 p.m. Tel: 01 406 2107

Tate Gallery, Millbank, SW1. Open weekdays 10.00 a.m. to 6.00 p.m., Sundays 2.00 p.m. to 6.00 p.m. Admission free. Tel: 01 821 1313. For details of special exhibitions recorded information is available on 01 821 7128

Theo Waddington Gallery,* 25 Cork Street, W1. Open Mondays to Fridays 10.00 a.m. to 5.30 p.m., Saturdays 10.00 a.m. to 1.00 p.m. Tel: 01 734 3534

Thumb Gallery,* 20/21 D'Arblay Street, W1. Open Mondays to Fridays 10.00 a.m. to 6.00 p.m., Saturdays 11.00 a.m. to 4.00 p.m. Tel: 01 434 2931

Waddington Galleries,* Gallery II, 34 Cork Street, W1. Gallery III, 4 Cork Street, W1. Waddington Graphics, 31 Cork Street, W1. Waddington Galleries 2 Cork Street, W1. Open Mondays to Fridays

10.00 a.m. to 5.30 p.m. Saturdays 10.00 a.m. to 1.00 p.m. Tel: 01 439 1866

Wallace Collection, Hertford House, Manchester Square, W1. Open weekdays 10.00 a.m. to 5.00 p.m., Sundays 2.00 p.m. to 5.00 p.m. Tel: 01 935 0687

Whitechapel Art Gallery, Whitechapel High Street, E1. Temporary exhibitions of contemporary art. Open daily (except Saturdays) 11.00 a.m. to 6.00 p.m. For details telephone 01 377 0107

Manchester   The City Art Gallery, Mosley Street, M2 3JL. Open weekdays 10.00 a.m. to 6.00 p.m. Admission free. Tel: 061 236 9422

The Gallery of Modern Art, Athenaeum, Princess Street. Open weekdays 10.00 a.m. to 6.00 p.m. Admission free. Tel: 061 236 9422

Whitworth Art Gallery, Oxford Road. Open weekdays 10.00 a.m. to 5.00 p.m. Admission free. Tel: 061 273 4865

Newcastle upon Tyne   Laing Art Gallery, Higham Place. Open Mondays to Saturdays 10.00 a.m. to 6.00 p.m., Sundays 2.30 p.m. to 5.30 p.m. Admission free. Tel: 0632 27734

The Hatton Gallery, The Quadrangle. Open weekdays 10.00 a.m. to 5.30 p.m. Admission free. Tel: 0632 28511

Norwich   Norwich Castle Museum, NRI 3JV, Open weekdays 10.00 a.m. to 5.00 p.m. Sundays 2.00 p.m. to 5.00 p.m. Admission charge. Tel: 0603 22233

Sainsbury Centre for the Visual Arts, University of East Anglia, NR4 7TJ. Open daily except Mondays 12.00 noon to 5.00 p.m. Tel: 0603 56060

Oxford   The Ashmolean Museum, Beaumont Street. Open Mondays to Saturdays 10.00 a.m. to 4.00 p.m., Sundays 2.00 p.m. to 4.00 p.m. Admission free. Tel: 0865 57522

Museum of Modern Art, Pembroke Street. Open Tuesdays to Saturdays, 10.00 a.m. to 5.00 p.m., Sundays 2.00 p.m. to 5.00 p.m. Admission free. Tel: 0865 722733

Plymouth   City Art Gallery, Drake Circus. Open weekdays 10.00 a.m. to 6.00 p.m. Admission free. Tel: 9752 68000

St Ives   Barbara Hepworth Museum, Barnoon Hill. Open weekdays 10.00 a.m. to 5.30 p.m. during the spring and summer. The museum closes at 4.30 p.m. during the winter months. Admission charge. Tel: 0736 796226

Sheffield   Graves Art Gallery, Surrey Street. Open weekdays 10.00 a.m. to 5.00 p.m. Admission free. Tel: 0742 734781

Mappin Art Gallery, Weston Park. Open weekdays 10.00 a.m. to 5.00 p.m., Sundays 2.00 p.m. to 5.00 p.m. Admission free. Tel: 0742 26281

Southampton   Art Gallery, Civic Centre. Open weekdays 11.00 a.m. to 5.45 p.m., Sundays 2.00 p.m. to 5.00 p.m. Admission free. Tel: 0703 23855

Wakefield   Art Gallery, Wentworth Terrace. Open weekdays 12.30 p.m. to 5.30 p.m., Sundays 2.30 p.m. to 5.30 p.m. Admission free. Tel: 0924 70211 Yorkshire Sculpture Park, Bretton Hall College, West Bretton, near Wakefield. Major exhibition of sculpture in an outdoor setting. Easy access from the M1, junction 38. Open Mondays to Fridays 10.00 a.m. to 6.00 p.m. Saturdays and Sundays 10.00 a.m. to 4.00 p.m. Admission charge. Tel: 092 485 261

Wolverhampton   Central Art Gallery, Lichfield Street. Open Mondays to Saturdays 10.00 a.m. to 6.00 p.m. Admission free. Tel: 0902 24549

Yeovil   Montacute House, Montacute TA 15 6XP (National Portrait Gallery Exhibition of Elizabethan and Jacobean Portraits). Open from April to October daily except Tuesdays from 12.30 p.m. to 6.00 p.m. Admission charge. Tel: Montacute 3289

York   City Art Gallery, Exhibition square. Open weekdays 10.00 a.m. to 5.00 p.m. Sundays 2.30 p.m. to 5.00 p.m. Admission charge. Tel: 0904 23839

Industry

Amberley   Chalk Pits Museum, Houghton Bridge, Amberley, West Sussex. A 14.5 ha (36-acre) open-air centre for industrial history. Open from Easter to October, Wednesdays to Sundays, 11.00 a.m. to 6.00 p.m. Admission charge. Tel: 079 881 370

Beamish, Co. Durham   North of England Open Air Museum. A 81 ha (200-acre) site containing reconstructions of buildings, a colliery, railway and farm, using the original materials and equipment. Open from April to September daily 10.00 a.m. to 6.00 p.m. From October to March the museum is closed on Mondays but open on other days 10.00 a.m. to 5.00 p.m. Admission charge. Tel: 0207 31811

Bristol   Bristol Industrial museum, Prince's Wharf, Bristol 2. Open Mondays to Wednesdays and Saturdays and Sundays 10.00 a.m. to 12.00 noon and 1.00 p.m. to 5.00 p.m. Tel: 9272 299771

Stoke-on-Trent   Chatterley Whitfield Mining Museum, Chatterley Whitfield Colliery, Turnstall, ST6 8UN. Open Tuesdays to Fridays 9.30 a.m. to 4.30 p.m., Saturdays and Sundays 10.00 a.m. to 5.00 p.m. Admission charge. Tel: 0782 813337.

Styal, Cheshire   Quarry Bank Mill. Open according to season, but normally Tuesdays to Sundays from 11.00 a.m. Admission charge.

Telford   Ironbridge Gorge Museums (Fig. 3.5). A major museum covering the period of the Industrial Revolution, spread over seven sites including a 17 ha (42-acre) open-air museum. Museum of the Year 1977 and European Museum of the Year 1978. Admission charges. Telephone 095 245 3522 for information on opening times.

Ulster   Ulster Folk and Transport Museum, Cultra Manor, Holywood BT18 OUE, Northern Ireland. A major folk and transport museum on a site of 178 acres about 13 km (8 miles) from Belfast. From May to September open weekdays 11.00 a.m. to 7.00 p.m., Sundays 2.00 p.m. to 7.00 p.m. From October to April the museum is open weekdays 11.00 a.m. to 5.00 p.m., Sundays 2.00 p.m. to 5.00 p.m. Admission charge. Tel: Holywood 5611

Photography

London   The Photographers Gallery, 5/8 Great Newport Street, WC2. Tel: 01 240 5511

Kodak Photographic Gallery, 190 High Holborn, WC1. Tel: 01 405 7841

Cardiff   The Photographic Gallery, 41 Charles Street. Tel: 0222 41667

York   Impressions, 14 Colliergate. Tel: 0904 54724

Historic collections of photographs are held by a number of museums and institutions including the Victoria and Albert Museum, London, the National Portrait Gallery, London, the Science Museum, London and the Royal Photographic Society, London. A National Museum of Photography, Film and Television is being developed at Bradford.

Sale-rooms

Good sources of material for visual research are available on viewing days at the major art auctioneers' sale-rooms in London and the

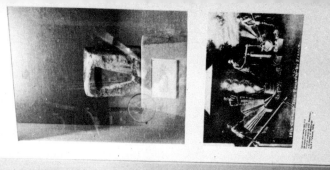

provinces. Admission is free and special viewing days are set aside for particular groups of items such as jewellery, books, paintings and furniture. The two leading international auctioneers, Christie's and Sotheby's, both publish excellent illustrated catalogues.

Christie's, 8 King Street, St James's London, SW1Y 6QT, Tel: 01 839 9060, and at 85 Old Brompton Road, South Kensington, SW7 3JS, Tel: 01 581 2231.
Christie's was founded in 1766 and has twenty-one specialist departments including Old Master Pictures, Water-colours, Drawings and Prints, Silver, English and European Ceramics and Glass, Jewellery, and Books, Manuscripts and Autograph Letters. A free valuation and an expert opinion is available on works of art brought to the reception desk. The premises at South Kensington specialise in the lower price range items and in new collecting fields such as nineteenth and twentieth century photographs, cigarette cards, dolls, toys and costumes. Details of sales are published in the national press.

Sotheby's, 34–35 New Bond Street, W1A 2AA, Tel: 01 493 8080, and at the Conduit Street Gallery, 26 Conduit Street, W1, and Bloomfield Place (Aeolian Hall), New Bond Street, W1A 2AA. There are also sale-rooms in Edinburgh and nine provincial centres.

The Bloomfield Place rooms specialise in books, manuscripts, coins, medals and jewellery. The Conduit Street Gallery deals with sales of items each Wednesday and Thursday which are normally under £1000. Viewing at this gallery continues until 7.30 p.m. on Mondays. Sotheby's offer a free sale-room estimate on items brought to their sale-rooms between 9.30 a.m. and 4.30 p.m. on any weekday. London sales are advertised in the national press.

Transport

Aysgarth, North Yorkshire   The Yorkshire Museum of Carriages and Horse Drawn Vehicles, York Mills, Aysgarth Falls. Open Easter to October. Daily 10.00 a.m. to 12.00 noon and 2.00 p.m. to 6.00 p.m. Admission charge.

Beaulieu   National Motor Museum, Beaulieu, Hampshire. Open weekdays and Sundays 10.00 a.m. to 6.00 p.m. Admission charge. Tel: 0590 612123.

Castle Donnington, Derby   The Donnington Collection Single-seater Grand Prix racing cars. Open daily 10.00 a.m. to 6.00 p.m. Admission charge. Tel: 0332 810048

Fig. 3.5   Ironbridge Gorge Museum – Museum of Iron Foundry Section

Crich, nr Matlock. The Tramways Museum. Open April to October on Saturdays and Sundays 10.30 a.m. to 5.00 p.m. From June to August also open on Tuesdays, Wednesdays and Thursdays 10.00 a.m. to 4.30 p.m.

Coventry The Museum of British Road Transport, Cooks Street. Major exhibition of cycles, motor cycles, cars and commercial vehicles. The museum's policy is to maintain all the exhibits in full working order. Open Tuesdays to Fridays 10.00 a.m. to 5.00 p.m., Saturdays 10.00 a.m. to 6.00 p.m. and Sundays 12.00 noon to 6.00 p.m. Admission charge. Tel: 0203 25555

Exeter Exeter Maritime Museum, The Quay. The largest collection of working boats on display in the world. The museum is open every day of the year except Christmas Day 10.00 a.m. to 6.00 p.m. from June to September, and 10.00 a.m. to 5.00 p.m. from October to May. Admission charge. Tel: 0392 58075

London London Transport Museum, Covent Garden, WC2. Open daily 10.00 a.m. to 6.00 p.m. Admission charge. Tel: 01379 6344 National Maritime Museum, Romney Road, Greenwich, SE10. Open weekdays 10.00 a.m. to 6.00 p.m.; Sundays 2.00 p.m. to 5.30 p.m. Admission free. The museum closes at 5.00 p.m. during the winter months. Tel: 01 858 4422

Royal Mews, Buckingham Palace Road, SW1. Open Wednesdays and Thursdays 2.00 p.m. to 4.00 p.m. (except Ascot week). Admission charge.

Stoke Bruerne, nr Towester The Waterways Museum. Open daily 10.00 a.m. to 6.00 p.m. from April to September, and 10.00 a.m. to 4.00 p.m. except Mondays from October to March. Admission charge. Tel: 0604 862229

Swindon Great Western Railway Museum, Farringdon Road. Open weekdays 10.00 a.m. to 5.00 p.m., Sundays 2.00 p.m. to 5.00 p.m. Admission charge. Tel: 0793 26161

Windermere Steamboat Museum, Rayrigg Road, Bowness-on-Windermere, Cumbria. Open weekdays Easter to October 10.00 a.m. to 5.00 p.m., Sundays 2.00 p.m. to 5.00 p.m. Admission charge. Tel: Windermere 5565

York National Railway Museum, Leeman Road. Open weekdays 10.00 a.m. to 6.00 p.m., Sundays 2.30 p.m. to 6.00 p.m. Admission charge. Tel: 0904 21261

Military

Bovington – Wareham The Tank Museum, Bovington Camp, Wareham, Dorset. Open weekdays 10.00 a.m. to 12.30 p.m. and 2.00 p.m. to 4.45 p.m. Tel: 0920 462721

Duxford, Cambridge Duxford Airfield, Duxford (a branch of the Imperial War Museum). Large collection of aircraft including Concorde. Open March to November daily 11.00 a.m. to 5.00 p.m. Admission charge. Tel: 0223 833963

London HMS *Belfast*, Symons Wharf, Vine Lane, SE1. Open daily summer 11.00 a.m. to 5.50 p.m., winter 11.00 a.m. to 4.30 p.m. Admission charge. Tel: 01 407 6434

Imperial War Museum, Lambeth Road, SE1. Open daily 10.00 a.m. to 5.50 p.m., Sundays 2.00 p.m. to 5.50 p.m. Admission free. Tel: 01 735 8922

The Museum of Artillery, Rotunda, Repository Road, Woolwich, SE18 4JJ. Open from April to October. Mondays to Fridays 10.00 a.m. to 12.45 p.m. and 2.00 p.m. to 5.00 p.m., Saturdays 10.00 a.m. to 12.00 noon and 2.00 p.m. to 5.00 p.m., Sundays 2.00 p.m. to 5.00 p.m. Admission free. Tel: 01 854 2424

National Army Museum, Royal Hospital Road, SW3. Open weekdays 10.00 a.m. to 5.30 p.m., Sundays 2.00 p.m. to 5.30 p.m. Admission free. Tel: 01 730 0717

Royal Air Force Museum, Aerodrome Road, Hendon, NW9, Open weekdays 10.00 a.m. to 6.00 p.m., Sundays 2.00 p.m. to 6.00 p.m. Major exhibition of aircraft.

Tower of London, Tower Hill, EC3. Open according to season, weekdays from 9.30 a.m. and Sundays from 2.00 p.m. Admission charge. Tel: 01 709 0765

Wellington Museum, Apsley House, Hyde Park Corner, W1. Open Tuesdays to Thursdays and Saturdays 10.00 a.m. to 6.00 p.m., Sundays 2.30 p.m. to 6.00 p.m. Tel: 01 499 5676

Portsmouth The Royal Naval Museum, HM Naval Base. Open weekdays 10.30 a.m. to 5.30 p.m., Sundays 1.00 p.m. to 5.00 p.m. Admission charge. Tel: 0705 22351

Wolverhampton RAF Aerospace Museum, Royal Air Force Cosford, WV7 3EX. Open Easter to October on Saturdays and Sundays 10.00 a.m. to 5.00 p.m. Admission charge. Tel: Albrighton 4872

Yeovilton Fleet Air Arm/Concorde Museum. Open weekdays 10.00 a.m. to 5.30 p.m., Sundays 12.30 p.m. to 5.30 p.m. Admission charge. Tel: Ilchester 840551

CHAPTER 4

Useful information for art and design students

4.1 ART AND DESIGN COURSES

Abbreviations used in this chapter and throughout.

DATEC   Design and Art Committee of the Business and Technician Education Council
CNAA   Council for National Academic Awards
BTEC   Business and Technician Education Council
UCCA   Universities Central Council on Admission
ADAR   Art and Design Admissions Registry

General information

The organisation of post-school education in the United Kingdom is broadly divided, for administration purposes, into further education, catering for the sixteen to nineteen age range, and higher education for the eighteen-plus age range. There is some considerable overlap between the two groups, and many colleges offer courses covering both further and higher education. The age at entry, academic qualifications, personal preferences and, for art and design applicants, an acceptable folio of work in art and design, normally determines the entry points to the system. It is generally possible to progress from one level to the next and to obtain additional qualifications.

Full-time courses in art and design

Normal minimum age at entry	Course
16	Foundation Course (2 years); DATEC Certificate or Diploma Course (2 years).
17	Foundation Course (1 year); DATEC Certificate or Diploma Course (1 year) with 50 per cent credit for previous experience.
18	DATEC Higher Certificate Course (1 year); DATEC Higher Diploma Course (2 or 3 years); Diploma of Higher Education Course (2 years);

CNAA First Degree Course (3 years);
CNAA first Degree (sandwich) Course (4 years)
University First Degree Course (3 years).
Master's Degree Course (1, 2 or 3 years).

Mature students are accepted on most courses subject to their fulfilling the entry requirements. Many courses are also available for part-time study.

Course validation and awards

There are two major validating organisations concerned with awards in art and design in England and Wales. The CNAA validates courses and makes awards for Degree and Diploma of Higher Education courses. The Business and Technician Education Council (BTEC), through its DATEC, validates courses and makes awards for Certificate, Diploma, Higher Certificate and Higher Diploma courses. Some universities also validate and make awards for art and design degree courses such as those at the Slade School and the Courtauld Institute of Art (University of London). The Royal College of Art is a postgraduate, university institution.

It is most important that applicants should obtain and study the prospectuses of the institutions that interest them before making any application. It is possible to visit some colleges before deciding on a final choice. Economic and other considerations affect the provision of education at all levels and may cause changes to be made in the provision of the courses which are outlined in this chapter. Evidence of creative potential is given particular emphasis for the majority of courses in art and design. The possession of the minimum entry qualifications does not, in itself, entitle an applicant to be admitted to a course.

Degree courses

The majority of degree courses in art and design are validated by the CNAA and take place in polytechnics. Full-time first degree courses are usually three years in length or four years if a 'sandwich' element in industry is included. Sandwich courses include a period spent in a relevant industry during which the student does not usually receive financial support from public funds. The normal minimum age for entry to degree courses is eighteen years. It is possible to study for some courses by part-time attendance. Entry requirements for degree courses vary, and it is therefore necessary to refer to the publications of the CNAA or UCCA who annually publish information and list all the available courses. The procedures for making an application also vary. All applications for CNAA art and design degree courses should normally be made to the Art and Design Admissions Registry, Imperial Chambers, 24 Widemarsh Street, Hereford, in January of the year of proposed entry to the course. A fee is payable. Students already attending a Foundation or DATEC Diploma or Certificate Course should obtain their application form from their college. Each applicant can list two colleges in order of preference and should also indicate an alternative to the second choice in case the named second-choice college has no vacancies. The processing of the forms is carried out by ADAR, but the individual colleges have the responsibility for all decisions on acceptances. Students who are not successful in obtaining their first, second or alternative choice are notified in June by ADAR of the remaining vacancies that exist. Applications for university courses should apply to UCCA, PO Box 28, Cheltenham, Gloucestershire GL 50 1HY, in the autumn of the year preceding intended entry to the course. A fee is payable. Students in schools and colleges should obtain their UCCA application forms through their tutors. The majority of university first degree courses are in fine art or the history of art, but degree courses are also available which combine other academic disciplines with art and design. The UCCA system enables a choice to be made of not more than five universities/colleges on an application form, naming one course of study at each or specifying alternative courses at the same institution. The processing of all applications is done by UCCA in the order of preference shown on the form, but the individual institution has the responsibility for all decisions on acceptances. If an applicant is not successful in obtaining one of the five choices shown on the form a clearing system is operated by UCCA in the late summer which informs all unplaced candidates of any vacancies that exist. Competition for both CNAA and university degree course places is very heavy. The universities only accept about 35 to 40 per cent of all applicants.

There are a number of degree courses which do not come within the registration schemes of either ADAR or UCCA. The majority of these courses lead to CNAA awards and are available in polytechnics. All applications for courses not listed in the annual publications of ADAR or UCCA should be made direct to the colleges offering the courses. Full details of the whole range of advanced courses in colleges of further and higher education are given in the *Compendium of Advanced Courses* published annually by the Regional Advisory Councils and obtainable from the London and Home Counties Regional Advisory Council for Technological Education, Tavistock House South, Tavistock Square, London WC1H 9LR. Telephone: 01 388 0027.

Diploma of Higher Education courses

These are two-year full-time or three-year part-time courses leading to a CNAA or university award. They are comparable in standard to the first two years of an Honours degree course and, although regarded as a qualification in their own right, are usually designed to enable students to transfer to a degree course with two years' credit. It is also possible to progress to certain professional qualifications. Entry requirements are similar to those for first degree courses, but intending applicants should obtain full details of the courses that interest them from the colleges concerned. Mature students are particularly catered for on many of these courses. The structure of Diploma of Higher Education courses varies, but generally the courses are of a modular or unit-based programme of study. The minimum age for entry is eighteen years. These courses are not available in Scotland.

Business and Technician Education Council (DATEC) courses
The majority of higher education courses in art and design, other than degree courses are now validated by the BTEC. The courses are known as DATEC courses and are available at colleges in England and Wales. There are two types of courses at this level. Higher Certificate courses, which normally last for one year of full-time study, and Higher Diploma courses, which are for two years of full-time study. Some Higher Diploma courses may last for three years and can include one year spent in a relevant industry. It is also possible to study for some awards on a part-time basis. Applicants for the higher awards must be over the age of eighteen years at entry and normally are expected to have previously completed a DATEC Diploma or Certificate course to the required standard. The courses are vocational in character and lead directly to employment opportunities. The Higher Diploma courses are, in general, based on analytical, interpretive and creative design practice, based on a broad development of both practical and organisational skills. Higher Certificate courses are generally planned to deal with specific developments of practical skills where the creative awareness is developed mainly through the use of processes and materials. Entry requirements vary and it is necessary to obtain full details of the courses from the colleges concerned. These courses are not available in Scotland. Applications for Higher Diploma courses must be made through ADAR (see pages 115/6).

Certificate/Diploma courses (DATEC)
These courses are available at a large number of colleges throughout England and Wales. Applications should be made direct to the college offering the course. The two types of course are different in character. Certificate courses are generally skills-based and develop creative awareness mainly through the use of materials and processes. Diploma courses are either generally broad-based or specific vocational courses or diagnostic courses which demand from the student analytical, interpretive and creative design practice based on a broad understanding of practical skills and related knowledge. The specific vocational courses can lead directly to employment opportunities or a more advanced course, while the diagnostic courses are planned to enable students to make an informed choice before applying for a Degree or Higher Diploma course. The minimum age for entry is sixteen years and for some courses it is possible to obtain credit for the first year, in which case the minimum age is seventeen years. Specific

courses are available in a wide range of disciplines. It is also possible to study for DATEC courses by part-time study. These courses are separately identified and are usually unit-based, enabling students to acquire the required number of units for an award over an unspecified period of time. The minimum academic entry requirements for DATEC Certificate and Diploma courses are passes in the Certificate of Secondary Education (CSE) examinations at Grade III in three subjects. Normally, however, applicants for Diploma courses in art and design are expected to have obtained passes in the General Certificate of Education 'O' level examinations in three subjects at either Grades A, B or C or the equivalent in CSE passes. In addition, applicants for both Certificate and Diploma courses are normally expected to submit a folio of their work in art and design. All students who have obtained a TEC Diploma or Certificate are eligible for possible entry to courses leading to both the Higher awards of the TEC and the awards of the CNAA in art and design.

Foundation courses
These are normally one-year courses of a diagnostic nature, planned, like the DATEC General Art and Design courses, to enable students to experience a wide range of disciplines over a short period of time to enable them to make an informed choice of a specialism for further study. The majority of these courses are pre-degree, the intention of the students being to progress to a first degree course. The minimum age at entry is usually seventeen years, but there are some two-year courses where the minimum age is sixteen. At the present time Foundation courses are not nationally validated, although many colleges offer an internal validation and external assessment leading to a college award. All applications should be made direct to the college offering the course. The academic entry qualifications are normally the same as for a first degree course.

Portfolio requirements for applicants to art and design courses
The majority of colleges offering courses in art and design require applicants to provide, usually at the interview stage, a portfolio of their own work with particular relevance to the course for which application has been made. Information on the recommended contents of the portfolio is usually sent to applicants with the letter inviting the candidate for interview, but some centres make a preliminary assessment based on the contents of a portfolio. The selection and presentation of the work is most important and a suitable folio case is very useful. Cases are available in A1, A2 and A3 sizes from several firms including Daler and Rotobord.

Open University courses
The Open University provides courses leading to the award of Bachelor of Arts (BA) degrees in a number of subjects of interest to students who

wish to study the History of Art and Design on a part-time basis. The courses are normally available for anyone over the age of twenty-one years. No previous academic qualifications are required. The University also offers individual courses for associate students in the history of art and design, but these courses do not lead to an award. Study is mainly home based and is supported by correspondence tuition and radio and television broadcasts. Each course successfully completed gains either a full or a half credit, depending on the time taken for the completion of the work. Each course lasts nine months and a full credit requires approximately ten to fifteen hours' work per week. A half credit covers the same amount of work spread over two weeks. A BA award is made to students who have obtained six full credits or the equivalent in full and half credits, and eight full credits are required for the award of a BA (Honours) degree. Most students take one full credit course per year and complete the BA programme in six years. The programme of study normally comprises a Foundation Course (not to be confused with Art and Design Foundation courses) followed by courses at second, third and possibly fourth levels. Courses from any of the six university faculties can be combined to form the programme for the final degree award. The University suggests the following courses for students in art history, but there are other related courses which may be substituted for those on the list:

An Arts Foundation Course
Seventeenth-century England
The Enlightenment
Modern Art and Modernism: Manet to Pollock
Art in Italy, 1480–1580
Arts and Society in Britain since the Thirties (project course)
Popular Culture

Applications for Open University degree courses should be made in January of the year preceding the proposed start of the course. All degree applications should be made to The Undergraduate Admissions Office, The Open University, PO Box 48, Milton Keynes MK7 6AB. Admissions and registration for an associate student course should be made to The Associate Student Central Office, The Open University, PO Box 76, Milton Keynes MK7 6AN.

The Royal College of Art

The College is a postgraduate university institution which awards the degrees of Master of Arts (RCA), Master of Design (RCA), PhD (RCA)., and Dr (RCA). Full-time Master's degree courses are available in the following subjects:

Automotive Design	Ceramics
Cultural History	Design Education
Design Research	Environmental design

Environmental Media
Film and Television
Glass
Graphic Information
Industrial Design
Painting
Print-making
Silversmithing

Fashion Design
Furniture Design
Graphic Design
Illustration
Jewellery
Photography
Sculpture
Textile Design

The College is organised in five faculties:
1. Applied Arts:
   (a) Ceramics and Glass;
   (b) Fashion Design;
   (c) Silversmithing and Jewellery;
   (d) Textile Design.
2. Painting, Sculpture and Environmental Media
3. Theoretical Studies:
   (a) Cultural History;
   (b) Design Education;
   (c) Design Research.
4. Three-dimensional design:
   (a) Environmental Design;
   (b) Furniture Design;
   (c) Industrial Design;
   (d) Management Studies.
5. Visual communication: Film and Television; Graphic Arts:
   (a) Graphic Design;
   (b) Graphic Communication;
   (c) Illustration;
   (d) Print-making;
   (e) Photography.

There are three research units: the Department of Design Research, the Textile Research Unit and the Graphic Information Research Unit. The majority of students follow courses of two or three years' duration leading to the Master's degree. Applications should be sent direct to the college.

Vocational part-time courses

Students who wish to study part-time for an examination in a vocational art and design subject, either because they need the qualification or because they wish to undertake the discipline of a structured course, have the choice of a wide range of subjects at all levels. All the major validating and awarding authorities including universities, CNAA and BTEC (DATEC) make awards to students who complete part-time courses. A large number of part-time courses are also available for students who wish to study for the awards of the City and Guilds of

London Institute, usually known as City and Guilds. University extra-mural departments, often in association with the Workers Educational Association (WEA), also provide courses. The level of vocational part-time courses varies from those that concentrate on the acquisition of craft skills in areas such as fashion, photography, jewellery, ceramics, furniture and printing to courses at undergraduate and postgraduate level. Fees for these courses are usually less than those for part-time recreational courses, but similar criteria often apply to the minimum numbers required for the initial enrolment. The mode of study also varies from part-time day only to part-time day and evening or part-time evening. Many courses allow for the examinations to be taken in stages to suit the convenience of the students, and courses leading to BTEC (DATEC) awards are often unit based which enables students to acquire individual units over an unspecified period of time.

Recreational part-time courses

Local Educational Authorities organise a wide range of courses during the day and evening for part-time recreational or non-vocational students. The majority of these courses are now self-financing, the cost of the lecturer and the running costs of the course being met from the fee income paid by the students. In order for this system to operate, each course must usually enrol a minimum number of students before it can start, and these initial enrolments can vary according to the nature of the course. In large urban areas such courses often take place in the local school or college of art and design or in colleges of further education. Sometimes evening courses are held in the art departments of local secondary schools. In rural areas courses may be held in village halls, junior schools or similar accommodation. Enrolment usually takes place once a year, in September, and courses usually meet once a week for three terms. The number of meetings can, however, vary from about thirty-six at the maximum to short courses of six, eight or ten meetings. Students normally have to provide all their own materials, and for some specialised activities such as pottery or jewellery payment of a studio fee is sometimes required. Information on the availability of courses is usually published in the local press, and details can often be obtained from local public libraries as well as from the local colleges.

Sotheby's courses

Sotheby's, the auctioneers, offer three full-time courses for students interested in a career in the buying and selling of works of art and also for those with a general interest in the history of art and design. The one-year, full-time course on works of art has the object of widening the visual experience of students and instilling a broad knowledge of a variety of objects of many periods. The Styles in Art Course is a thirteen-week, full-time course intended to give students a good introduction to the stylistic developments in the fine and decorative arts of Europe. Lastly, the nineteenth- to twentieth-century Decorative Works of Art Course is a thirteen-week, full-time course for students who wish to specialise in the European decorative arts of the nineteenth and twentieth centuries. Applications should be made to Sotheby's, 34–35 New Bond Street, London W1A 2AA.

Degree courses: Diploma of Higher Education courses: CNAA

Multidisciplinary courses

The following courses embrace more than one field in art and design and are, therefore, listed separately from courses in specific areas of study. In this section FT = full-time, PT = part-time, HE = higher education. Full details of entry requirements are shown on pages 145–146. The addresses of all colleges listed in this handbook are shown in Section 4.6

Bradford College: BA, FT – 3 years. Art and Design: students choose to study two areas from the following three: textile media, two-dimensional design (visual communication) and three-dimensional design, and also two from fine arts, community arts and design.

Cambridgeshire College of Arts and Technology: BA Honours, FT – 3 years, PT and/or mixed mode – 4/6 years. Humanities/Social Studies.

Crewe and Alsager College of Higher Education: Dip. HE FT – 2 years PT – 3/6 years.

BA, FT – 3 years Combined Studies (Crafts): subjects include ceramics, graphic design, print-making and typography, jewellery, photography, textiles and wood.

Dartington College of Arts: Dip. HE, FT – 2 years. Art and Design in Social Contexts: the course adopts a different approach to art and design in education or other social contexts from the traditional training of specialised designers or fine artists, and is appropriate for students who may wish to pursue further studies leading to a B.Ed. degree or enter careers in community arts or similar fields.

Duncan of Jordanstone College of Art: BA/BA Honours, FT – 4 years. Design: ceramics, graphic design, illustration, interior design, jewellery and silversmithing, printed textiles, product design and woven textiles.

BA/BA Honours, FT – 4 years. Fine Art (Painting and Sculpture): the course includes both fine art and design elements. In years 2, 3 and 4 students specialise in drawing and painting or sculpture.

Glasgow School of Art: BA/BA Honours, FT – 4 years. Art: the first year of the course includes both fine art and design elements. In years

2, 3 and 4 students may specialise in painting, print-making, sculpture, murals or stained glass, or may pursue studies in all of these. A complementary design subject may be studied by arrangement.

BA/BA Honours, FT – 4 years. Design: The first year includes both fine art and design elements, after which students specialise in one of the following: ceramics, embroidered and woven textiles, furniture/interior/product design, graphic design, printed textiles or silversmithing and jewellery. Complementary studies in design or fine art may be arranged.

London College of Printing: BA Honours (sandwich), 4 years. Media and Production Design: studies include photography, visual research and analysis, typography and letter design, printing processes and techniques. In the second year and beyond, options are publicity design, information design and communication media design.

North Staffordshire Polytechnic: BA Honours, FT – 3 years. Design: major study specialisms are typographic design, audio-visual design, illustration, photography, domestic products, industrial tableware and holloware, printed surface pattern, designer/craftsman ceramics, architectural and sculptural ceramics and designer/craftsman glass.

Robert Gordon's Institute of Technology: BA/BA Honours, FT –4 years. Design and Craft: in the first year students take a range of subjects which include design and crafts, drawing and painting, sculpture and print-making. In year 2 fine art subjects are discontinued. In years 3 and 4 students select two subjects from ceramics, graphic design, jewellery, printed textiles and woven textiles with the option of dropping one in the fourth year. Woven textiles is approved as a main study subject at degree level only.

BA/BA Honours, FT – 4 years. Fine Art: in the first year students take a range of subjects which include design and crafts, drawing and painting, sculpture and print-making. In year 2 design and crafts are discontinued. In years 3 and 4 drawing and painting or sculpture is studied with an option of a supporting subject.

West Midlands College of Higher Education: BA FT – 3 years. Visual Communications Studies: the media covered in this course include audio-visual, graphic design and photography.

Fine art

A fine art course may be based on the traditional activities of painting, sculpture, drawing and print-making, or it may encourage the students to use other media or combinations of media. In either case, a course in this area is likely to be relatively open-ended, taking its direction from the creative development of the individual student. All courses contain elements of critical and theoretical studies, including the history of art and design.

Bath Academy of Art: BA Honours, FT – 3 years.
City of Birmingham Polytechnic: BA Honours, FT – 3 years.
Brighton Polytechnic: BA Honours, FT – 3 years.
Bristol Polytechnic: BA Honours, FT – 3 years.
Camberwell School of Art and Crafts: BA Honours, FT – 3 years.
Canterbury College of Art: BA Honours, FT – 3 years.
Central School of Art and Design: BA Honours, FT – 3 years.
Chelsea School of Art: BA Honours, FT – 3 years.
Coventry (Lanchester) Polytechnic: BA Honours, FT – 3 years.
Duncan of Jordanstone College of Art: BA/BA Honours, FT – 4 years.
Exeter College of Art and Design: BA Honours, FT – 3 years.
Falmouth School of Art: BA Honours, FT – 3 years.
Glasgow School of Art: BA/BA Honours FT – 4 years. Art.
Gloucestershire College of Arts and Technology: BA Honours, FT – 3 years.
Goldsmith's College: BA Honours, FT – 3 years.
Gwent College of Higher Education: BA Honours, FT – 3 years
Hull College of Higher Education: BA Honours, FT – 3 years.
Kingston Polytechnic: BA Honours, FT – 3 years.
Leeds Polytechnic: BA Honours, FT – 3 years.
Leicester Polytechnic: BA Honours, FT – 3 years.
Liverpool Polytechnic: BA Honours, FT – 3 years.
Loughborough College of Art and Design: BA Honours, FT – 3 years
Maidstone College of Art: BA Honours, FT – 3 years.
Manchester Polytechnic: BA Honours, FT – 3 years.
Middlesex Polytechnic: BA Honours, FT – 3 years.
Newcastle upon Tyne Polytechnic: BA Honours, FT – 3 years.
North-East London Polytechnic: BA Honours, FT – 3 years.
North Staffordshire Polytechnic: BA Honours, FT – 3 years.
Norwich School of Art: BA Honours, FT – 3 years.
Portsmouth Polytechnic: BA Honours, FT – 3 years.
Preston Polytechnic: BA Honours, FT – 3 years.
Ravensbourne College of Art and Design: BA Honours, FT – 3 years
Robert Gordon's Institute of Technology: BA/BA Honours, FT – 4 years.
St Martin's School of Art: BA Honours, FT – 3 years.
Sheffield City Polytechnic: BA Honours, FT – 3 years.
South Glamorgan Institute of Higher Education: BA Honours, FT – 3 years.
Stourbridge College of Technology and Art: BA Honours, FT – 3 years.
Sunderland Polytechnic: BA Honours, FT – 3 years.
Trent Polytechnic: BA Honours, FT – 3 years.
Ulster Polytechnic: BA Honours, FT – 3 years.
West Surrey College of Art and Design: BA Honours, FT – 3 years.
Wimbledon School of Art: BA Honours, FT – 3 years.
Winchester School of Art: BA Honours, FT – 3 years.
The Polytechnic, Wolverhampton: BA Honours, FT – 3 years.

Graphic design

Graphic design courses are mainly concerned with visual communication, particularly the techniques and disciplines that have to do with design for print, e.g. typography, graphic reproduction and illustration. To these, many add an introduction (and some add more than an introduction) to film and television graphics. Some courses place an emphasis on subjective illustration, some on information graphics, some on publicity and advertising. All courses contain an element of complementary studies, including the history of art and design. Some related courses are listed in the section on Art and design multidisciplinary courses.

Bath Academy of Art: BA Honours, FT – 3 years.
City of Birmingham Polytechnic: BA Honours, FT – 3 years.
Brighton Polytechnic: BA Honours, FT – 3 years.
Bristol Polytechnic: BA Honours, FT – 3 years.
Camberwell School of Art and Crafts: BA Honours, FT – 3 years.
Canterbury College of Art: BA Honours, FT – 3 years.
Central School of Art and Design: BA Honours, FT – 3 years.
Chelsea School of Art: BA Honours, FT – 3 years.
Coventry (Lanchester) Polytechnic: BA Honours, FT – 3 years.
Duncan of Jordanstone College of Art: BA/BA Honours, FT – 4 years, Design.
Exeter College of Art and Design: BA honours, FT – 3 years.
Glasgow School of Art: BA/BA Honours FT – 4 years. Design.
Gwent College of Higher Education: BA Honours, FT – 3 years.
Harrow College of Higher Education/The Polytechnic of Central London: BA Honours, FT – 3 years. Graphic Information Design.
Hull College of Higher Education: BA Honours, FT – 3 years.
Kingston Polytechnic: BA Honours, FT – 3 years.
Leeds Polytechnic: BA Honours, FT – 3 years.
Leicester Polytechnic: BA Honours, FT – 3 years.
Liverpool Polytechnic: BA Honours, FT – 3 years.
London College of Printing: BA Honours, FT – 3 years.
Maidstone College of Art: BA Honours, FT – 3 years.
Manchester Polytechnic: BA Honours, FT – 3 years. Design for Learning is included as an option in this graphic design course.
Middlesex Polytechnic: BA Honours, FT – 3 years.
BA Honours (sandwich) – 4 years. Scientific and Technical Illustration.
Newcastle upon Tyne Polytechnic: BA Honours, FT – 3 years.
North Staffordshire Polytechnic: BA Honours, FT – 3 years. Design.
Norwich School of Art: BA Honours, FT – 3 years.
Plymouth Polytechnic/Cornwall Technical College: BA Honours, FT (sandwich) – 4 years. Scientific and Technical Graphics.
Preston Polytechnic: BA Honours (sandwich) – 4 years.
Ravensbourne College of Art and Design: BA Honours, FT – 3 years.

Robert Gordon's Institute of Technology: BA/BA Honours, FT – 4 years. Design and Craft.
St Martin's School of Art: BA Honours, FT – 3 years.
Trent Polytechnic: BA Honours, FT – 3 years. Information Graphics.
Ulster Polytechnic: BA Honours, FT – 3 years.
West Midlands College of Higher Education: BA, FT – 3 years. Visual Communications Studies.
The Polytechnic, Wolverhampton: BA Honours, FT – 3 years.

History of art and design

These courses concentrate mainly on the modern period. The opportunity to engage in some practical studio work occurs, the aim of which is to support the historical studies and deepen the student's understanding of the work of the artist and the designer. There are no specific entry requirements for these courses, and applications should be addressed direct to the polytechnic offering the course and not through the Art and Design Admissions Registry. History of art and design also appears as an option in certain Arts and Humanities and Multidisciplinary courses. For further information on such courses consult the *CNAA Directory* (see Bibliography, p. 157).
Brighton Polytechnic: BA Honours, FT – 3 years. History of Design.
Leicester Polytechnic: BA/BA Honours, FT – 3 years. History of Art and Design in the Modern Period.
Manchester Polytechnic: BA Honours, FT – 3 years. History of Design.
Newcastle upon Tyne Polytechnic: BA/BA Honours, PT – 5 years. History of Modern Art, Design and Film.
BA/BA Honours, FT – 3 years. History of Modern Art, Design and Film.
North Staffordshire Polytechnic: BA Honours, FT – 3 years. History of Design and the Visual Arts.
Sheffield City Polytechnic: BA Honours, FT – 3 years. History of Art, Design and Film.

Photography, film and television

These courses are specialist first degree courses. Some Fine Art and Graphic Design courses also contain studies in photography and film/video. Entry requirements for these courses vary and applicants are advised to obtain the institutions' prospectuses for details.
The Polytechnic of Central London: BA Honours, FT – 3 years. Film and Photographic Arts: subjects include visual studies, aesthetics and communication studies.
BSc/BSc Honours, FT – 3 years. Photographic Sciences: the course provides two options – photographic technology and scientific photography – and is designed for those wishing to work on the scientific side of the photographic industry or as scientific photographers in industry or government.

Derby Lonsdale College of Higher Education: BA Honours, FT – 3 years. Photographic Studies: the course is a practical visual arts course with photography and allied subjects as the principal means of expression.

Harrow College of Higher Education/Middlesex Polytechnic: BA Honours, FT – 3 years. Applied Photography, Film and Television: students study technical theory and also aesthetics and sociology which are used to develop awareness of the value and place of photography, film and television in comparison with other media. Options include cultural and commercial applications of photography and scientific and industrial applications of photography, film and television.

BA, PT – 2 years. Photographic Media Studies: the course is designed to allow holders of the Professional Qualifying Examination of the Institute of Incorporated Photographers (IIPPQE) to read for a degree.

London College of Printing: BA Honours, FT – 3 years. Visual Communication: Photography, Film and Television: the course provides a broad education in visual communications, developing theoretical, technical and professional skills and knowledge. Specialisation in either photography or film and television is possible in the later stages.

Trent Polytechnic: BA Honours, FT – 3 years. Photography: the course is concerned with the study and exploration of the fundamental nature of photography, of how equipment and materials currently available determine its potential and how conventions of quality and previous usage affect the understanding of photographs.

West Midlands College of Higher Education: BA, FT – 3 years. Visual Communications Studies (see under Art and Design Multidisciplinary courses.)

West Surrey College of Art and Design: BA Honours, FT – 3 years. Photography, Film and Video, Animation.

Textiles/fashion

In the area of textiles/fashion, colleges are approved to conduct courses in 'chief studies' and supporting studies, e.g. fashion, embroidery, woven and printed textiles. As in other art and design courses, courses in textiles/fashion contain an element of complementary studies, including the history of art and design. Visits to fashion and textile centres abroad are encouraged; for students whose chief study is fashion, they are obligatory. Applicants to the sandwich course at Huddersfield must possess English and mathematics at GCE 'O' level.

City of Birmingham Polytechnic: BA Honours, FT – 3 years. Chief studies: embroidery, fashion, woven and printed textiles.

Brighton Polytechnic: BA Honours (sandwich) – 4 years. Fashion, Textiles Design and Administration.

Bristol Polytechnic: BA Honours, FT – 3 years. Chief study: fashion.

Camberwell School of Art and Crafts: BA Honours, FT – 3 years. Chief study: woven and printed textiles.

The Polytechnic of Central London/Harrow College of Higher Education: BA Honours, FT – 3 years. Chief Study Fashion.

Central School of Art and Design: BA Honours, FT – 3 years. Chief study: woven and printed textiles.

Duncan of Jordanstone College of Art: BA/BA Honours, FT – 4 years. Design (see also multidisciplinary courses).

Glasgow School of Art: BA/BA Honours, FT – 4 years. Design (see also multidisciplinary courses).

Gloucestershire College of Arts and Technology: BA Honours, FT – 3 years. Chief study: fashion.

Goldsmiths' College: BA Honours, FT – 3 years. Chief study: embroidery.

The Polytechnic Huddersfield: BSc Honours (sandwich) – 4 years. Textile Design.

Kidderminster College of Further Education/The Polytechnic Wolverhampton: BA Honours (sandwich) – 4 years. Design of Carpets and Related Textiles.

Kingston Polytechnic: BA Honours, FT – 3 years. Chief study: fashion.

Leicester Polytechnic: BA Honours, FT – 3 years. Chief studies: fashion, woven and printed textiles, contour fashion, footwear design.

Liverpool Polytechnic: BA Honours, FT – 3 years. Chief studies: fashion, woven and printed textiles.

Loughborough College of Art and Design: BA Honours, FT – 3 years. Chief studies: embroidery, woven and printed textiles.

Manchester Polytechnic: BA Honours, FT – 3 years. Chief studies: fashion, embroidery, woven and printed textiles.

Middlesex Polytechnic: BA Honours, FT – 3 years. Chief studies: fashion, woven and printed textiles.

Newcastle upon Tyne Polytechnic: BA Honours (sandwich) – 4 years. Fashion.

North East London Polytechnic: BA Honours (sandwich) – 4 years. Fashion with Marketing.

North Staffordshire Polytechnic: BA Honours, FT – 3 years. Design (see also multidisciplinary courses).

Preston Polytechnic: BA Honours (sandwich) – 4 years. Fashion.

Ravensbourne College of Art and Design: BA Honours, FT – 3 years. Chief study: fashion.

Robert Gordon's Institute of Technology: BA/BA Honours, FT – 4 years. Design and Craft (see also multidisciplinary courses).

St Martin's School of Art: BA Honours, FT – 3 years. Chief study: fashion.
BA Honours (sandwich) – 4 years. Fashion.

Scottish College of Textiles: BA Honours, FT – 4 years. Industrial Design (Textiles).

Trent Polytechnic: BA Honours, FT – 3 years. Chief studies: fashion, textile design.

BA Honours (sandwich) – 4 years. Knitwear Design.
Ulster Polytechnic: BA Honours, FT – 3 years. Chief studies: embroidery, woven and printed textiles.
West Surrey College of Art and Design: BA Honours, FT – 3 years. Chief study: woven and printed textiles.
Winchester School of Art: BA Honours, FT – 3 years. Chief study: woven and printed textiles.

Three-dimensional design

In the area of three-dimensional design, colleges are approved to conduct courses in 'chief studies'. Examples of chief studies are furniture design, ceramics and interior design. In some cases, a course has been approved which is an amalgam; wood/metal/ceramics/plastics, for example. Where colleges offer courses in more than one chief study in the three-dimensional design area, some treat them as quite separate courses, while some offer a course which begins as a general course and divides at some point to focus on particular chief studies. All courses in this area contain a supporting study or studies and complementary studies, including the history of art and design.

Bath Academy of Art: BA Honours, FT – 3 years. Chief study: ceramics.
City of Birmingham Polytechnic: BA Honours, FT – 3 years. Chief studies: ceramics with glass, furniture, industrial design (engineering), interior design, jewellery and silversmithing, theatre design.
Brighton Polytechnic: BA Honours, FT – 3 years. Chief studies: interior design, wood/metal/ceramics/plastics.
Bristol Polytechnic: BA Honours, FT – 3 years. Chief studies: ceramics, wood, metal and plastics.
Buckinghamshire College of Higher Education: BA Honours, FT – 3 years. Chief studies: ceramics with glass, furniture, interior design, silver/metal.
Camberwell School of Art and Crafts: BA Honours, FT – 3 years. Chief studies: ceramics, silver/metal.
Central School of Art and Design: BA Honours, FT – 3 years. Chief studies: ceramics, industrial design (engineering), jewellery, theatre design.
City of London Polytechnic: BA Honours (sandwich) – 4 years. Silversmithing, Jewellery and Allied Crafts.
Coventry (Lanchester) Polytechnic: BA Honours (Sandwich) – 4 years. Industrial Design Transportation.
Duncan of Jordanstone College of Art: BA/BA Honours, FT – 4 years. Design (see also multidisciplinary courses).
Glasgow School of Art: BA/BA Honours, FT – 4 years. Design (see also multidisciplinary courses).

Kingston Polytechnic: BA Honours, FT – 3 years. Chief studies: furniture, interior design.

Leeds Polytechnic: BA Honours, FT – 3 years. Chief studies: furniture, industrial design (engineering), interior design.

Leicester Polytechnic: BA Honours, FT – 3 years. Chief studies: ceramics, furniture, industrial design (engineering), interior design, silversmithing.

Loughborough College of Art and Design: BA Honours, FT – 3 years. Chief studies: ceramics, furniture, silversmithing and jewellery.

Manchester Polytechnic: BA Honours, FT – 3 years. Chief studies: industrial design (engineering), interior design, wood/metal/ceramics.

Middlesex Polytechnic: BA Honours, FT – 3 years. Chief studies: ceramics, furniture, silver/metal.
BA Honours (sandwich) – 4 years. Interior design.
BA Honours (sandwich) – 4 years. Jewellery and Ceramics.

Napier College: BSc (sandwich) – 4 years. Industrial Design (Technology)

Newcastle upon Tyne Polytechnic: BA Honours, FT – 3 years. Design Craftsmanship.
BA Honours, (Sandwich) – 4 years. Design for Industry, Wood, Metal and Plastics.

The Polytechnic of North London: BA, FT – 3 years. Interior Design.

North Staffordshire Polytechnic: BA Honours, FT – 3 years. Design (see also multidisciplinary courses).

Ravensbourne College of Art and Design: BA Honours, FT – 3 years. Chief studies: furniture, wood/metal/ceramics/plastics.

Robert Gordon's Institute of Technology: BA/BA Honours, FT – 4 years. Design and Craft (see also multidisciplinary courses).

Sheffield City Polytechnic: BA Honours, FT – 3 years. Chief studies: industrial design (engineering), silversmithing and jewellery.

Polytechnic of the South Bank: BA Honours (sandwich) – 4 years. Engineering Product Design.

South Glamorgan Institute of Higher Education: BA Honours, FT – 3 years. Chief studies: ceramics, industrial design.

Stourbridge College of Technology and Art: BA Honours, FT – 3 years. Chief study: glass.

Teesside Polytechnic: BA Honours, FT – 3 years. Chief studies: industrial design (engineering), interior design.

Trent Polytechnic: BA Honours, FT – 3 years. Chief study: theatre design.
BA Honours (sandwich) – 4 years. Furniture Design.
BA Honours (sandwich) – 4 years. Interior Design.

Ulster Polytechnic: BA Honours, FT – 3 years. Chief studies: ceramics, furniture, interior design, silversmithing and jewellery.

West Surrey College of Art and Design: BA Honours, FT – 3 years. Chief studies: ceramics, glass, metals.

Wimbledon School of Art: BA Honours, FT – 3 years. Chief study: theatre design.

The Polytechnic, Wolverhampton: BA Honours, FT – 3 years. Chief studies: ceramics, wood/metal/plastics.

DATEC (BTEC) courses

The DATEC validated courses listed may be subject to alteration or amendment. Full information on the availability of all DATEC courses may be obtained from the offices of the BTEC or from the colleges. The courses are shown under broad subject groupings and the full title of the course may vary from that given in this handbook.

Higher National Diploma courses: DATEC

Design
South Glamorgan Institute of Higher Education. FT – 2 years.
Stockport College of Technology. FT – 2 years.
West Sussex College of Design, Worthing. FT – 2 years.

Design Crafts
Chesterfield College of Art and Design/Derby Lonsdale College of Higher Education (joint). FT – 2 years.
Cumbria College of Art and Design, Carlisle. FT – 2 years.
Epsom School of Art and Design. FT – 2 years.
Medway College of Design, Rochester. FT – 2 years.
Preston Polytechnic. FT – 2 years.

Graphic design/Visual communication/Illustration/Advertising Design
Amersham College of Further Education. FT – 2 years.
Barnet College/Middlesex Polytechnic. FT – 2 years.
Barnfield College/Dunstable College (joint). FT – 2 years.
Berkshire College of Art and Design. FT – 2 years.
Bournemouth and Poole College of Art and Design. FT – 2 years.
Cambridgeshire College of Arts and Technology. FT – 2 years.
Cleveland College of Art and Design. FT – 2 years.
Colchester Institute. FT – 2 years.
Cornwall Technical College. FT – 2 years.
Croydon College. FT – 2 years.
Cumbria College of Art and Design. FT – 2 years.
Derby Lonsdale College of Higher Education. FT – 2 years.
Dewsbury and Batley Technical and Art College. FT – 2 years.
Doncaster Metropolitan Institute of Higher Education. FT – 2 years.
Ealing College of Higher Education. FT – 2 years.
East Ham College of Technology. FT – 2 years.

Epsom School of Art and Design. FT – 2 years.
Granville College/Sheffield Polytechnic. FT – 2 years.
Great Yarmouth College of Art and Design. FT – 2 years.
Hounslow Borough College. FT – 2 years.
Jacob Kramer College, Leeds. FT – 2 years.
Lincolnshire College of Art, Lincoln. FT – 2 years.
London College of Printing. FT – 2 years.
Loughborough College of Art and Design. FT – 2 years.
Medway College of Design, Rochester. FT – 2 years.
Nene College, Northampton. FT – 2 years.
Newcastle upon Tyne College of Arts and Technology. FT – 2 years.
North East Wales Institute of Higher Education, Wrexham. FT – 2 years.
Plymouth College of Art and Design. FT – 2 years.
Richmond upon Thames College. FT – 2 years.
Salford College of Technology. FT – 2 years.
Salisbury College of Art. FT – 2 years.
Somerset College of Arts and Technology. FT – 2 years.
Southampton College of Higher Education. FT – 2 years.
Southend-on-Sea College of Technology. FT – 2 years.
The Suffolk College of Higher and Further Education. FT – 2 years.
Sunderland Polytechnic. FT – 2 years.
The College, Swindon. FT – 2 years.
Watford College. FT – 2 years.
York College of Arts and Technology. FT – 2 years.

Technical illustration
Blackpool and Fylde College of Further and Higher Education. FT – 2 years.
Bournemouth and Poole College of Art and Design. FT – 2 years.
Cornwall Technical College, Redruth. FT – 2 years.
Portsmouth College of Art, Design and Further Education. FT – 2 years.
West Glamorgan Institute of Higher Education, Swansea. FT – 2 years.

Photography
Blackpool and Fylde College of Further and Higher Education. FT – 2 years.
Gwent College of Higher Education, Newport. FT – 2 years.
Manchester Polytechnic. FT – 2 years.
Medway College of Design, Rochester. FT – 2 years.
Salisbury College of Art. FT – 2 years.
West Glamorgan Institute of Higher Education, Swansea. FT – 2 years.

Photography/Film/Television
Bournemouth and Poole College of Art and Design. FT – 2 years.

Printing

London College of Printing. FT – 2 years.
Trent Polytechnic, Nottingham. FT – 2 years.
Watford College. FT – 2 years.

Fashion (including fashion/textile design)

Berkshire College of Art and Design. FT – 2 years.
Bournemouth and Poole College of Art and Design. FT – 2 years.
Cleveland College of Art and Design. FT – 2 years.
Derby Lonsdale College of Higher Education. FT – 2 years.
Dewsbury and Batley Technical and Art College. FT – 2 years.
Epsom School of Art and Design. FT – 2 years.
London College of Fashion. FT – 2 years.
Loughborough College of Art and Design. FT – 2 years.
Medway College of Design, Rochester. FT – 2 years.
Salford College of Technology. FT – 2 years.

Stage Management

Central School of Speech and Drama, London. FT – 2 years.

Textile design

Blackburn College of Technology and Design. FT – 2 years.
Chelsea School of Art. FT – 2 years.
Derby Lonsdale College of Higher Education. FT – 2 years.
Huddersfield Polytechnic. FT – 2 years.
Somerset College of Arts and Technology, Taunton. FT – 2 years.

Three-dimensional design and crafts

Berkshire College of Art and Design. FT – 2 years.
Chelsea School of Art. FT – 2 years.
Colchester Institute. FT – 2 years.
Epsom School of Art and Design. FT – 2 years.
Medway College of Design, Rochester. FT – 2 years.
Portsmouth College of Art, Design and Further Education. FT – 2 years.

Spatial design including interior, exhibition and environmental design

Bournemouth and Poole College of Art and Design. FT – 2 years.
Dewsbury and Batley Technical and Art College. FT – 2 years.
Humberside College of Higher Education. FT – 2 years.
Hull College of Higher Education. FT – 2 years.
London College of Furniture. FT – 2 years.
Medway College of Design, Rochester. FT – 2 years.
Newcastle College of Arts and Technology. FT – 2 years.

Ceramics including studio pottery
Derby Lonsdale College of Higher Education/Chesterfield College of Art and Design. FT – 2 years.
Cornwall Technical College, Redruth. FT – 2 years.
Croydon College. FT – 2 years.
Harrow College of Higher Education. FT – 2 years.
Preston Polytechnic. FT – 2 years.
Stafford College of Further Education. FT – 2 years.
West Glamorgan Institute of Higher Education, Swansea. FT – 2 years.

Architectural stained glass
West Glamorgan Institute of Higher Education, Swansea. FT – 2 years.

Conservation crafts and archaeology
Dorset Institute of Higher Education. FT – 2 years.

Conservation of fine art/Restoration
City and Guilds of London Art School
Gateshead Technical College. FT – 2 years.

Mural design
Chelsea School of Art. FT – 2 years.

Paper conservation/book restoration/Fine art conservation
Camberwell School of Arts and Crafts. FT – 2 years. (Paper/Book)
Gateshead Technical College. FT – 2 years (Fine Art)

Theatre production and design
Croydon College. FT – 2 years.

Theatre wardrobe and design
Mabel Fletcher Technical College, Liverpool. FT – 2 years.

Higher National Certificate courses: DATEC

Design crafts
Southampton College of Higher Education (ceramics). FT – 1 year.

Fashion
Croydon College. FT – 1 year.
York College of Arts and Technology. FT – 1 year.

Graphic design
Stafford College of Further Education. FT – 1 year.

Photography
Richmond upon Thames College. (P/T)

Printing
Kitson College, Leeds.
Manchester Polytechnic (P/T)

Technical Graphic Design
Barnsfield College/Dunstable College. FT – 1 year.

Technical Communication
Blackpool and Fylde College of Further and Higher Education. FT – 1 year

Technical illustration
Blackpool and Fylde College of Further and Higher Education. FT – 1 year.
Bourneville College of Art and Design. FT – 1 year.

BTEC (DATEC) National Diploma and Certificate courses

The following courses generally require two years of full-time study from the minimum age at entry of sixteen years.

Diploma courses
Audio-visual studies
Dewsbury and Batley Technical and Art College.
Epsom School of Art and Design.
Harrogate College of Arts and Adult Studies.
North-East Wales Institute of Higher Education, Wrexham.

Ceramics
West Glamorgan Institute of Higher Education, Swansea.
Harrogate College of Arts and Adult Studies.

Conservation crafts
Lincolnshire College of Art and Design, Lincoln.
North East Wales Institute of Higher Education, Wrexham.

Design
Dyfed College of Art.
Kitson College, Leeds (with Photography/Printing)

Design crafts
Cornwall Technical College, Redruth.
Medway College of Design, Rochester.
Nene College, Northampton.
Plymouth College of Art and Design.
Rycotewood College, Thame and North Oxford Technical College.
Southampton College of Higher Education (Dip./Cert.)

Display design
Bradford College.
Granville College, Sheffield.
Havering Technical College (Dip./Cert.).
Hertfordshire – Cassio College, Watford/Ware College
Hounslow Borough College.
Jacob Kramer College, Leeds.
Mabel Fletcher College, Liverpool.
Medway College of Design, Rochester.
Plymouth College of Art and Design.
Southend-on-Sea College of Technology.
Southgate Technical College.
Tameside College of Technology, Ashton-under-Lyme.
Trowbridge College.
Ware College/Cassio College, Watford.

Display and exhibition design
College for the Distributive Trades, London.
Newcastle upon Tyne College of Arts and Technology.

Exhibition and interior design
Bradford College.
Dewsbury and Batley Technical and Art College.
Trowbridge Technical College.

Exhibition/museum design
Hastings College of Further Education.
Hull College of Higher Education.

Fashion
Barnfield College, Luton.
Berkshire College of Art, Maidenhead.
Bournemouth and Poole College of Art and Design.
Bradford College.
Cauldon College, Stoke-on-Trent.
Chesterfield College.
Coventry Technical College.
Croydon College.
Derby Lonsdale College of Higher Education.
Dewsbury and Batley Technical and Art College.
Doncaster Metropolitan Institute of Higher Education.
East Warwickshire College of F, E. Rugby.
Epsom School of Art and Design.
Gloucestershire College of Arts and Technology.
Granville College, Sheffield.
Great Yarmouth College of Art and Design.
Gwent College of Higher Education, Newport.

Hastings College of Further Education.
Hounslow Borough College.
Jacob Kramer College, Leeds.
Leicester: Southfields College of Further Education.
London College of Fashion.
Loughborough College of Art and Design.
Medway College of Design, Rochester.
Nene College, Northampton.
Newcastle Upon Tyne College of Arts and Technology.
Plymouth College of Art and Design.
Salisbury College of Art.
Southampton College of Further Education (Dip./Cert.).
South Fields College of Further Education, Leicester.
Stafford College of Further Education.
Tameside College of Technology, Ashton-under-Lyne.
West Nottinghamshire College, Mansfield.
West Sussex College of Design, Worthing.
Wigan College of Technology.
York College of Arts and Technology.

Fashion and textile design
Canterbury College of Art.
Southend-on-Sea College of Technology.
Southport College of Art and Design.

Footwear design
Cordwainers Technical College, London.

General art and design
Accrington and Rossendale College.
Amersham College of Further Education.
Barnet College.
Barnfield College, Luton.
Barnsley College.
Blackburn College of Technology and Design.
Bournemouth and Poole College of Art and Design.
Bournville School of Art and Crafts, Birmingham.
Braintree College.
Burnley College of Technology.
Colchester Institute of Higher Education.
Chelsea School of Art.
Chesterfield College of Art and Design.
Cleveland College of Art and Design, Middlesbrough.
Croydon College.
Eastbourne College of Further Education.
East Ham College of Technology.
East Warwickshire College.

Epsom School of Art and Design.
Granville College, Sheffield.
Great Yarmouth College of Art and Design.
Harlow Technical College.
Havering Technical College.
Herefordshire College of Art and Design, Hereford.
Hounslow Borough College.
Huddersfield Technical College.
Isle of Ely College of Further Education and Horticulture.
Leek College of Further Education.
Leigh College.
Lincolnshire College of Art and Design, Lincoln.
Loughton College.
Mabel Fletcher Technical College, Liverpool.
Newcastle under Lyme College.
North Devon Technical College, Barnstaple.
North Warwickshire College of Technology and Art, Nuneaton.
North Worcestershire College/Redditch College of Further Education.
Reigate School of Art.
Richmond upon Thames College.
Rotherham College.
Salford College.
Scarborough Technical College.
Solihull College of Further Education.
Somerset College of Arts and Technology, Taunton.
Southend-on-Sea College of Technology.
Southport College of Art and Design.
Southwark College, London.
Stourbridge College of Art and Technology.
Suffolk College of Higher Education and Further Education, Ipswich.
Sutton Coldfield College of Further Education.
Thurrock College.
Walsall College of Art.
W. R. Tuson College, Preston.
Wakefield College.
West Bridgford College of Further Education.
West Nottinghamshire College of Further Education, Mansfield.
West Glamorgan Institute of Higher Education, Swansea.
Worcester Technical College.

General vocational design

Bolton Metropolitan College.
Chesterfield College.
Cleveland College of Art and Design, Middlesbrough.
Cornwall Technical College, Redruth.
Croydon College.

Cumbria College of Art and Design, Carlisle.
Darlington College.
Derby Lonsdale College of Higher Education.
Ealing College of Higher Education.
Eastbourne College of Further Education.
Herefordshire College of Art and Design, Hereford.
Hertfordshire Joint Scheme:
    Hertfordshire College of Art and Design, St Albans; Stevenage College.
    Watford College.
Mid-Warwickshire College of Further Education, Leamington Spa.
Monskwearmouth College of Further Education.
North-East Wales Institute of Higher Education, Wrexham.
Salford College.
South Shields Marine and Technical College.
Southwark College, London.
West Sussex College of Design, Worthing.
Worcester Technical College.

Graphic design/Visual communication
Barnfield College, Luton/Dunstable College.
Berkshire College of Art and Design, Maidenhead.
Blackpool and Fylde College of Further and Higher Education.
Bournemouth and Poole College of Art and Design.
Bradford College.
Brunel College.
Canterbury College of Art and Design.
Central Liverpool College of Further Education.
Chesterfield College of Art and Design.
Croydon College.
Colchester Institute of Higher Education.
Cornwall Technical College, Redruth.
Derby Lonsdale College of Higher Education.
Dewsbury and Batley Technical and Art College.
Doncaster Metropolitan Institute of Higher Education.
Durham: New College.
East Ham College of Technology.
Epsom School of Art and Design.
Great Yarmouth College of Art and Design.
Harlow Technical College.
Hastings College of Further Education.
Hounslow Borough College.
Isle of Ely College of Further Education and Horticulture.
Jacob Kramer College, Leeds.
Lincolnshire College of Art and Design, Lincoln.
Liverpool Central College.
London College of Printing.
Loughborough College of Art and Design.

Medway College of Design, Rochester.
Nene College, Northampton.
Newcastle upon Tyne College of Arts and Technology.
North-East Wales Institute of Higher Education, Wrexham.
Plymouth College of Art and Design.
Portsmouth College of Art, Design and Adult Studies.
Rotherham College of Arts and Community Studies.
Salisbury College of Art.
Scarborough College.
Granville College, Sheffield.
South Devon Technical College, Torquay.
Southend-on-Sea College of Technology.
Southampton College of Higher Education.
Southport College of Art and Design.
Stafford College of Further Education.
Stockport College of Technology.
Stourbridge College of Art and Technology.
Suffolk College of Higher Education and Further Education, Ipswich.
Swansea: West Glamorgan Institute of Higher Education.
Swindon: The College.
Tameside College of Technology, Ashton-under-Lyne.
Wakefield College of Higher Education.
West Glamorgan Institute of Higher Education, Swansea.
West Nottinghamshire/West Bridgford Colleges of Further Education.
Wigan College of Technology.
York College of Arts and Technology.

Graphic design/book design
Harlow Technical College.

Graphic communication
Gloucester College of Arts and Technology.

Illustration
Ravensbourne College of Art and Design, Bromley.

Interior design
South Devon Technical College.
Trowbridge Technical College.
Willesden College of Technology.

Interior and furnishing studies
London College of Furniture.

Jewellery design
Bradford College.
Epsom School of Art and Design.

Jewellery/silversmithing
North East Wales Institute of Higher Education, Wrexham.

Medical photography
West Bromwich College of Technology.

Paper conservation
Camberwell School of Art and Crafts.

Photography
Barking College of Technology.
Berkshire College of Art and Design, Maidenhead.
Dewsbury and Batley Technical and Arts College.
Granville College, Sheffield.
Harrogate College of Arts and Adult Studies.
W. R. Kitson College, Leeds.
Newcastle upon Tyne College of Arts and Technology.
Plymouth College of Art and Design.
Richmond upon Thames College.
Southport College.
Tameside College of Technology, Ashton-under-Lyne.
West Bromwich College.
West Glamorgan Institute of Higher Education, Swansea.
Wigan College of Technology.

Print, design and production
Southampton College of Higher Education.

Printing
Watford College.
West Bridgford College of Further Education.

Restoration studies
City and Guilds School of Art, London.

Scientific illustration
Southampton College of Higher Education.

Spatial design
Midway College of Design, Rochester

Surface pattern design
Dewsbury and Batley Technical and Arts College.
Granville College, Sheffield.
Jacob Kramer College, Leeds.
Stockport College of Technology.

Technical illustration
Blackpool and Fylde College of Further and Higher Education.
Bournemouth and Poole College of Art and Design.
Maidenhead.
Cornwall Technical College, Redruth.
Doncaster Metropolitan Institute of Higher Education.
Portsmouth College of Art and Design.
West Glamorgan Institute of Higher Education, Swansea.

Three-dimensional design
Berkshire College of Art and Design, Maidenhead.
Cleveland College of Art and Design, Middlesbrough.
Colchester Institute of Higher Education.
North Warwickshire College of Technology and Art, Nuneaton.
Portsmouth College of Art and Design.
Stafford College of Further Education.
West Glamorgan Institute of Higher Education, Swansea.
York College of Arts and Technology.

Three-dimensional design – product design
West Sussex College of Design, Worthing.

Three-dimensional design – theatre/television
West Sussex College of Design, Worthing.

Textile design
Bradford College.
Great Yarmouth College of Art and Design.
West Sussex College of Design, Worthing.

Typographic Design
Blackburn College of Technology and Design.

Visual communication
West Sussex College of Design, Worthing.
Wirral College of Art and Design, Birkenhead.

Certificate courses – audio visual
Openshaw Technical College, FT and PT.

Design crafts
Rycotewood College, Thame.

Design for clothing
Herefordshire College of Art and Design, Hereford.
Somerset College of Arts and Technology, Taunton.

Display
Bootle-Hugh Baird College of Further Education.
Isle of Ely College of Further Education and Horticulture.
Uxbridge College.
Windsor and Maidenhead College of Further Education.

Engineering illustration
Barnfield College, Luton

Fashion
Bournville School of Arts and Crafts, Birmingham.
Boston College of Further Education.
Cauldon College, Stoke-on-Trent.
Leek College of Further Education.
Mid-Warwickshire College, Leamington Spa.
North East Wales Institute of Higher Education, Wrexham.
Redbridge College, London.
Scarborough College.
Waltham Forest College.
Wigan College of Technology.

Fashion (light clothing)
Cleveland College of Art and Design, Middlesbrough.

General vocational design
Lowestoft College of Further Education.
Sutton Coldfield College.

Graphic design
Bournville School of Art and Crafts, Birmingham.
East Warwickshire College.
Exeter College of Art and Design.
Farnborough Technical College, PT.
Isle of Ely College of Further Education and Horticulture.
Mabel Fletcher/Central Colleges, Liverpool.
Mid-Cheshire College, Northwich.
Northumberland Technical College.
North Warwickshire College, Nuneaton.
Percival Whitley College, Halifax.
Solihull College.
Southfields College of Further Education, Leicester.
Sutton Coldfield College of Further Education.
Walsall College of Art.
Ware College
Wigan College of Technology (studio techniques)

Jewellery
Wirral Metropolitan College.

Learning resources
Belfast College of Technology. PT.
Harrogate College of Arts and Adult Studies. PT.
South Thames College, London.

Technical illustration
Bath Technical College.
Bournville School of Art and Crafts, Birmingham.
Isle of Ely College.
Mid-Cheshire College, Northwich.
Richmond upon Thames College.

Three-dimensional design
Bournville School of Arts and Crafts, Birmingham.
Jacob Kramer College, Leeds

Photography
Bournville School of Arts and Crafts, Birmingham.
Mid-Cheshire College, Northwich.
Paddington College, London.
Ware College.
Wigan College of Technology.
Wirral Metropolitan College.

Photographic laboratory skills/techniques
Blackpool and Fylde College of Further and Higher Education.
Kingsway Princeton College, London.

Printing

Certificate in Design for Print
Barnfield College/Dunstable College (joint)

Certificate in Printing
Brunel Technical College, Bristol. PT.
Central Liverpool College of Further Education. PT
Colchester Institute. PT and FT
Hong Kong – Kwun Tong Technical Institute. PT and FT
Kitson College Leeds. PT
London College of Printing. PT
Manchester Polytechnic. PT
Matthew Boulton Technical College, Birmingham. PT
Norwich City College of Further and Higher Education. PT

Southampton College of Higher Education. PT
Watford College. (Reprography)
Watford College. PT
West Bridgford College of Further Education. PT

Entry requirements

CNAA First Degree entry requirements: art and design

The normal, minimum qualifications for entry to a full-time or sandwich course leading to the award of a CNAA First Degree in the area of art and design is as follows:

- (a) A General Certificate of Education with passes in five subjects, including two subjects at Advanced level.
- or (b) A General Certificate of Education with passes in four subjects, including three subjects at Advanced level.
- or (c) A Scottish Certificate of Education with passes in five subjects, of which three are at the higher grade.
- or (d) A Scottish Certificate of Education with passes in four subjects, all at the higher grade.
- or (e) An Ordinary National Certificate or Diploma at a good standard.
- or (f) The satisfactory completion of a full-time Foundation Course in art and design of not less than one academic year in length, together with one of the following:
    - (i) A General Certificate of Education with passes in five subjects at ordinary level.
- or (ii) A General Certificate of Education with passes in four subjects including one at Advanced level.
- or (iii) Such qualifications as the Council considers to be acceptable in lieu of (i) and (ii) above.
- or (g) Such other qualifications as the Council deems to be acceptable in lieu of those specified in (a) to (f) above, i.e. a BTEC Certificate or Diploma in Art and Design in appropriate subjects as specified by, or acceptable to, the relevant Board or Committee of the Council, together with a portfolio of work or other comparable evidence of achievement demonstrating degree potential.

    In the selection of students for courses in art and design, the Council will expect that emphasis will normally be placed upon evidence of creative ability in art and design and, for the purpose of demonstrating this evidence, the completion of a Foundation Course in art and design, as specified in (f) above represents the preferred entry qualification for full-time courses in art and design in England, Wales and Northern Ireland.

    A student shall not normally be admitted to any full-time or sandwich course in England, Wales or Northern Ireland unless he or she will have attained the age of eighteen years by 31 December in the year of entry. An institution may also exercise its discretion to admit a student whose qualifications do not conform to the standard minimum entrance requirements, but who presents other evidence which, in the opinion of the institution, indicates that he or she has the capacity and attainment to pursue the course of study proposed, provided that the proportion of students thus admitted is not so large as to affect significantly the nature and presentation of the course.

An institution may admit a mature student aged twenty-one years or over by 31 December in the year of entry, to the beginning of a course, not specifically designed for such a student, even when he or she does not possess the normal course entry qualifications, provided that the institution is first satisfied that the student has the necessary motivation, potential and knowledge to follow the course successfully.

CNAA Diploma of Higher Education entry requirements
The Council's normal minimum requirements for entry to Diploma of Higher Education courses are the same as those outlined above for First Degree courses.

Note: Passes at Grade I in the Certificate of Secondary Education are acceptable in place of grades A, B or C at Ordinary level in the General Certification of Education.

Full details of the regulations governing admission to CNAA courses are contained in *The Principles and Regulations for the Award of the Council's First Degrees and Dip. H.E. (1979)* and the Council's *Directory of First Degree and Diploma of Higher Education Courses* published annually by the CNAA.

BTEC (DATEC) Higher Diploma and Higher Certificate course entry requirements

Length of programmes   Although BTEC programmes can be taken by any mode of study and can, therefore, vary in length, the normal duration for students with the minimum entry qualification is:
1. *Higher Diploma:* two years full-time or two or three years by sandwich study.
2. *Higher Certificate:* two years day-release, possibly less by block-release. One year full-time.

Admission to programmes   Under the BTEC's policy of credit exemption, students can be admitted to programmes at different ages and with different levels of attainment. The BTEC specifies the normal entry requirements for each programme, examples of which are given below:

Higher Diploma: the appropriate BTEC Certificate or Diploma or equivalent qualifications.

Although the entry qualifications of the students may vary, the final BTEC awards gained have a common standard. The minimum age for entry to a Higher Diploma or Higher Certificate programme is eighteen years. In the majority of cases applicants for BTEC (DATEC) courses are required to provide a folio of work in art and design or other comparable evidence of achievement demonstrating potential for the course. In some cases students who have successfully completed a Foundation course may be eligible for entry to a Higher Certificate or Higher Diploma programme.

Some colleges will specify particular BTEC Diploma or Certificate awards as entry qualifications to their Higher Certificate or Higher Diploma programmes. It is therefore important that applicants should obtain from the colleges full details of the courses in which they are interested.

BTEC (DATEC) Diploma and Cetificate course entry requirements

Length of programmes
1. *Diploma:* two years full-time, two or three years by sandwich study. study.
2. *Certificate:* three years by day-release, possibly less by block release. Two years full-time.

Admission to programmes   The BTEC specifies the normal entry requirements for each programme, examples of which are given below:
1. *Diploma:* ranges from CSE Grade III passes in three relevant subjects to three GCE 'O' level passes at Grade C, according to the needs of the students and the industry catered for in the programme.
2. *Certificate:* the minimum requirement is often Grade III passes in CSE.

Although the entry qualifications of the students may vary, the final BTEC awards gained have a common standard.

A large number of Diploma courses in the art and design area require three passes at GCE 'O' level as a minimum entry requirement. In the majority of cases applicants for BTEC (DATEC) courses are required to provide a folio of work in art and design or other comparable evidence of achievement demonstrating potential for the course. The normal, minimum age for entry to Certificate and Diploma courses is sixteen years.

Foundation Course entry requirements
These courses are not nationally validated and there is no national pattern of entry requirements. In general the one-year, seventeen-plus

age at entry courses require academic standards comparable to those needed for a First Degree of the CNAA. The two-year courses starting at age sixteen usually require less than the minimum CNAA entry requirements, but sometimes provide opportunities for students to gain additional academic qualifications during the course.

4.2 GLOSSARY

Art and design

Airbrush A device for spraying paint with compressed air.

Art Nouveau Nineteenth-century ornamental art-style.

Assemblage A three-dimensional form made from two or more components.

Collage A work put together by the assembly of individual, two-dimensional or three-dimensional elements.

Contour The edge or edges of an object, normally, but not necessarily, three-dimensional.

Composition The bringing together of several elements to make a whole.

Display type Displayed typesetting, such as title-pages, advertisements, etc. distinguished from solid text setting.

End grain A cross-section of timber. Used for wood engraving.

Ergonomics The study of work in relation to the environment in which it is performed.

Fine art Painting, sculpture, etc. – work of a non-utilitarian nature in which mind and imagination are chiefly concerned.

Floppy disk Flexible disk coated with a magnetic substance used to store data for a computer.

Form As in 'human form'. The visual relationship between two or more three-dimensional shapes.

Half-tone Representation of light and shade photographically by dots of different sizes. Used for all the usual printing methods.

Hologram A means of optical imaging without the use of lenses, now a practical reality with the advent of the laser (see below).

House style The customary style of spelling, capitalisation, etc. followed in a printing or publishing establishment.

Laser Light Amplification by Stimulated Emission of Radiation. A coherent light source using a crystalline solid (e.g. ruby) liquid or gas-discharge tube, in which atoms are pumped simultaneously into excited states by an incoherent light flash.

Line As in 'line drawing'. An idea or observation expressed by a drawn line without the use of tone (shading).

Logo Shortened form of 'logotype', a word or several letters cast in one piece of type, or presented as a trade mark.

Mass Large undefined shape. Usually three-dimensional

Microprocessor A very small computer (composed of 1 or more integrated circuits functioning as a unit).

Monochrome Work in a number of tones of the same colour.

Monoprint A single colour print.

Nodal point Usually a drawing which plots the surface of an object with changes in direction shown as points, dots or nodes.

Object-trouve Found objects utilised as artefacts by being incorporated into an art work.

Offset printing Process in which the ink from a plate is received on a rubber-covered blanket cylinder, from which it is transferred to the paper or other material.

Pattern Usually associated with surface design. Can be regular or irregular, two- or three-dimensional.

Photogram Photographic image made direct on to photographic paper without the use of a negative.

Plane A flat, level surface.

Portfolio A collection of drawings, prints etc.

Rag-mould Paper making process utilising rag.

Resist A coating of chemically neutral substance placed over a surface when the latter has to be protected at some stage of processing as in etching or selective dyeing.

Reverse printing Where the negative image is reversed in processing to give a positive image.

Scale Size, in relation to other objects.

Silhouette An object or person viewed two-dimensionally and drawn without variation in colour or tone.

Software General term for programming or compiling accessories used for computing or data-processing systems.

Source material Original material used to develop an idea.

Space The three-dimensional area between two or more defined forms.

Structure The underlying components which influence the external appearance.

Tactile The 'feel' or texture of a surface when the response is not gained from actually touching but by being conscious of the nature of the texture.

Tension breaker Liquid for increasing the flow of acrylic colours on non-absorbert surface.

Texture Surface quality, i.e. rough, smooth, wet, oily, prickly, etc.

Tone As 'tone drawing'. An idea or observation expressed in gradations of one or more colours.

Toothed surface Roughened surface, usually to paper.

Trichromatic separation Three-colour separation.

Volume The extent of a three-dimensional space occupied or enclosed within an object.

4.3 PAPER SIZES

International standard paper sizes

The three basic sheets of the international standard series are known as 'A', 'B' and 'C', which are related by a common dimensional ratio extending from 'A' to the larger sheets 'B' and 'C'. Sizes obtained from subdivisions of these sheets are designated by numerals following the sheet letter (A4, B6, C2, etc). Each numeral indicates a halving of the previous area. Thus, A1 is half, A2 a quarter and A3 an eighth of the A sheet area, and so on. Full sheet sizes are coded A0, B0, C0. For still larger sizes, the numeral is prefixed to the letter. Thus, 2A is twice the size of A0.

The 'A' Series (illustrated below) is designed for all standard printing and stationary purposes – that is, for the whole range of printed forms, catalogues and periodicals, and for all administrative, commercial and technical documents or letterheads.

Dimensions of 'A' sheet sizes are listed below. Note that these are all *trimmed* sizes, which ensures consistency of supply however many different suppliers are involved.

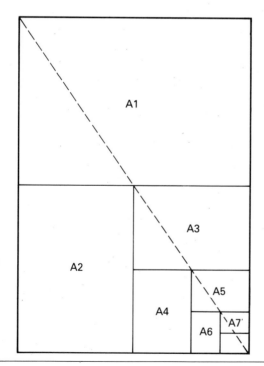

Fig. 4.1

	millimetres	*inches (approx.)*
A0	841 × 1189	$33\frac{1}{8} \times 46\frac{3}{4}$
A1	594 × 841	$23\frac{3}{8} \times 33\frac{1}{8}$
A2	420 × 594	$16\frac{1}{2} \times 23\frac{3}{8}$
A3	297 × 420	$11\frac{3}{4} \times 16\frac{1}{2}$
A4	210 × 297	$8\frac{1}{4} \times 11\frac{3}{4}$
A5	148 × 210	$5\frac{7}{8} \times 8\frac{1}{4}$
A6	105 × 148	$4\frac{1}{8} \times 5\frac{7}{8}$
A7	74 × 105	$2\frac{7}{8} \times 4\frac{1}{8}$

Imperial paper sizes

crown	15×20 in
demy	$17\frac{1}{2} \times 22\frac{1}{2}$ in
foolscap	$17 \times 13\frac{1}{2}$ in
imperial	22×30 in
medium	18×23 in
post	$12\frac{1}{2} \times 15\frac{1}{2}$ in
royal	20×25 in
small royal	25×19 in

4.4 METRIC/IMPERIAL MEASUREMENTS AND EQUIVALENTS

Table 4.1 Metric/imperial measures

Metric measures and equivalents

Length

1 millimetre (mm)		= 0.0394 in
1 centimetre (cm)	= 10 mm	= 0.3937 in
1 metre (m)	= 100 cm	= 1.0936 yd
1 kilometre (km)	= 1,000 m	= 0.6214 mile

Area

1 sq cm (cm²)	= 100 mm²	= 0.1550 in²
1 sq metre (m²)	= 10,000 cm²	= 1.1960 yd²
1 sq km (km²)	= 100 hectares	= 0.3861 mile²

Volume/Capacity

1 cu. cm (cm³)		= 0.0610 in³
1 cu. decimetre (dm³)	= 1,000 cm³	= 0.0353 ft³
1 cu. metre (m³)	= 1,000 dm³	= 1.3080 yd³
1 litre (l)	= 1 dm³	= 1.76 pt
		= 2.113 US 1 pt
1 hectolitre (hl)	= 100 l	= 21.997 gal
		= 26.417 US gal

Mass (Weight)

1 milligram (mg)		= 0.0154 grain
1 gram (g)	= 1,000 mg	= 0.0353 oz
1 metric carat	= 0.2 g	= 3.0865 grains
1 kilogram (kg)	= 1,000 g	= 2.2046 lb
1 tonne (t)	= 1,000 kg	= 0.9842 ton
		= 1.1023 short ton

Imperial measures and equivalents

Length

1 inch (in)		= 2.54 cm
1 foot (ft)	= 12 in	= 0.3048 m
1 yard (yd)	= 3 ft	= 0.9144 m
1 mile	= 1,760 yd	= 1.6093 km

Area

1 sq inch (in²)		= 6.4516 cm²
1 sq foot (ft²)	= 144 in²	= 0.0929 m²
1 sq yard (yd²)	= 9ft²	= 0.8361 m²
1 acre	= 4,840 yd²	= 4046.9 m²
1 sq mile (mile²)	= 640 acres	= 2.590 km²

Volume/Capacity

1 cu inch (in³)		= 16.387 cm³
1 cu foot (ft³)	= 1,728 in³	= 0.0283 m³
1 cu yard (yd³)	= 27 ft³	= 0.7646 m³
1 fluid ounce (fl oz)		= 28.413 ml
1 pint (pt)	= 20 fl oz	= 0.5863 l
1 gallon (gal)	= 8 pt	= 4.546 l

Mass (Weight)

1 ounce (oz)	= 437.5 grains	= 28.35 g
1 pound (lb)	= 16 oz	= 0.4536 kg
1 stone	= 14 lb	= 6.3503 kg
1 hundredweight (cwt)	= 112 lb	= 50.802 kg
1 ton	= 20 cwt	= 1.016 t

Table 4.2 Approximate equivalents

Length centimetres (cm)		inches (in)	Mass (Weight) kilograms (kg)		pounds (lb)
2.54	1	0.394	0.454	1	2.205
5.08	2	0.787	0.907	2	4.409
7.62	3	1.181	1.361	3	6.614
10.16	4	1.575	1.814	4	8.819
12.70	5	1.969	2.268	5	11.023
15.24	6	2.362	2.722	6	13.228
17.78	7	2.756	3.175	7	15.432
20.32	8	3.150	3.629	8	17.637
22.86	9	3.543	4.082	9	19.842
25.40	10	3.937	4.536	10	22.046
50.80	20	7.874	9.072	20	44.092
76.20	30	11.811	13.608	30	66.139
101.60	40	15.748	18.144	40	88.185
127.00	50	19.685	22.680	50	110.231
152.40	60	23.622	27.216	60	132.277
177.80	70	27.559	31.752	70	154.324
203.20	80	31.496	36.287	80	176.370
228.60	90	35.433	40.823	90	198.416
254.00	100	39.370	45.359	100	220.462

Length kilometres (km)		miles	Volume litres		UK gallons
1.609	1	0.621	4.546	1	0.220
3.219	2	1.243	9.092	2	0.440
4.828	3	1.864	13.638	3	0.660
6.437	4	2.485	18.184	4	0.880
8.047	5	3.107	22.730	5	1.100
9.656	6	3.728	27.276	6	1.320
11.265	7	4.350	31.822	7	1.540
12.875	8	4.971	36.368	8	1.760
14.484	9	5.592	40.914	9	1.980
16.093	10	6.214	45.460	10	2.200
32.187	20	12.427	90.919	20	4.399
48.280	30	18.641	136.379	30	6.599
64.374	40	24.855	181.839	40	8.799
80.467	50	31.069	227.298	50	10.998
96.561	60	37.282	272.758	60	13.198
112.654	70	43.496	318.217	70	15.398
128.748	80	49.710	363.677	80	17.598
144.841	90	55.923	409.137	90	19.797
160.934	100	62.137	454.596	100	21.997

4.5 BIBLIOGRAPHY

Books

(a) Painting

Doerner, M. (1969) *The Materials of the Artist*. Harrap, London.
Kay, R. (1961) *The Painters' Guide to Studio Methods and Materials*. Studio Vista, London; Doubleday, New York.

(b) Colour

Birren, F. (Ed.) 1970. *The Elements of Colour* (Itten). Van Nostrand Reinhold, New York.

(c) Sculpture

Mills, J. (1976) *The Techniques of Sculpture*. Batsford, London.

(d) Print-making

Gilmour, P. (1981) *Artists in Print*. BBC Publications.

Heller, J. (1972) *Printmaking Today*. Holt, Rinehart & Winston, New York.

Mara, T. (1979) *Screen Printing*. Thames & Hudson, London.

Vicary R. (1976) *Lithography*. Thames & Hudson, London.

(e) Graphic design

Craig, J. (1974) *Production for the Graphic Designer*. Pitman Publishing, London; Watson-Guptill Publications, New York.

Garland K. (1966) *Graphics Handbook*. Studio Vista, London; Reinhold, New York.

Garland, K. (1980) *Illustrated Graphics Glossary*. Barrie & Jenkins, London.

Hurlburt, A. (1977) *Layout – The Design of the Printed Page*. Barrie & Jenkins, London; Watson–Guptill Publications, New York.

Hurlburt, A. (1978) *The Grid*. Van Nostrand Reinhold, New York.

Lewis, J. (1977) *Typography – Design and Practice*. Barrie & Jenkins, London.

(f) Photography

Feininger, A. (1978) *The Complete Photographer*. Thames & Hudson, London.

J. Hedgecoe and M. J. Langford (1971) *Photography – Materials and Methods*. Oxford University Press.

Horder, A. (Ed.) (1971) *Manual of Photography*. Lund Humphries, London; Focal Press, New York.

Langford, M. J. (1977) *Basic Photography*. Focal Press.

(g) Fashion

J. Arnold (1972) *Patterns of Fashion*. Macmillan, London; Drama Books Specialists, USA.

(h) Textiles

Dushemin, M. (1975) *Handweaving*. Batsford, London.

Hardingham, M. (1978) *The Illustrated Dictionary of Fabrics*. Studio Vista/Cassell, London; Collier-Macmillan, New York.

Russ, S. (1964) *Fabric Printing by Hand*. Studio Vista, London; Watson-Guptill Publications, New York.

Storey, J. (1974) *Textile Printing*. Thames & Hudson, London.

(i) Geramics
M. Billington and J. Colbeck (1974) *The Techniques of Pottery*. Batsford, London.

(j) Jewellery/silversmithing
Brynner, I. (1968) *Modern Jewelry*. Van Nostrand Reinhold, New York.
Gentille, T. (1973) *Jewellery*. Evans Bros., London.
Smith, K. (1975) *Practical Silversmithing and Jewelry*. Studio Vista, London.

(k) Art and design history
Clark, K. (1949) *Landscape into Art*. John Murray, London.
Gombrich, E. H. (1950) *The Story of Art*. Phaidon, London.
Murray, P. and L. (1959) *A Dictionary of Art and Artists*. Penguin Books, Harmondsworth.
Wilenski, R. H. (1940) *Modern French Painters*. Faber & Faber, London.
Wolfflin, H. (1952) *Classic Art*, Phaidon, London.

Monographs and series

There are a number of very good monographs on the work of individual artists, and also books dealing with the major periods of art history or aspects of the art of countries and continents which are usually available as part of a series of books published over a period of time.

The following series are particularly recommended for the quality of the reproductions.

Hofstatter, H. (Gen. Ed.) *Panorama of World Art Series*. Harry N. Abrams, London, New York. Titles available include: *Art of the Late Middle Ages; Pre-Columbian Art and Later Indian Tribal Art; African and Oceanic Art; Art of the Far East; Baroque and Rococo Art; Renaissance and Mannerist Art*.
H. Jaffe and Busignani (Gen. Eds) *Twentieth Century Masters Series*. Hamlyn.
Lecaidano, P. (Ed.) *Classics of World Art Series*. Weidenfeld and Nicolson, London; Harry N. Abrams, New York.
Phaidon *Colour Plate Series*.
Skira Series, The Treasures of Asia and *Great Centuries of Painting*. Some titles are also available in a new edition published by Macmillan.
The *World of Art Library*. Thames & Hudson, London.

Visual research
Betjeman, J. (Ed.) (1979) *Collins Guide to Parish Churches of England and Wales*. Collins, London.
R. Fedden and J. Kenworthy-Brown (1979) *The Country House Guide*. Jonathan Cape, London

Fry, P. S. (1980) *The David and Charles Book of Castles*, David & Charles, Newton Abbot.

Pevsner, N. (Founding Ed.) *The Buildings of England* (Series). Penguin Books, Harmondsworth.

Museum and Galleries in Great Britain and Ireland. Published annually by ABC Historic Publications.

Periodicals

Audio-visual
Audio-Visual Monthly

Ceramics
Ceramic Review, bi-monthly.

Design
The Architectural Review, monthly; *Domus* (Italy), monthly; *Design Magazine* (UK), monthly.

Fashion
Fashion Weekly; *Robes Couture* (France), twice yearly; *Vogue UK*, monthly.

Film
British Film Institute Monthly Film Bulletin; Framework, quarterly; *Sight and Sound*, quarterly.

Fine arts
Art forum (USA), monthly; *Art International* (Swiss), five per year; *Art Monthly* (UK); *Artscribe* (UK), bi-monthly; *Arts Review* (UK), Fortnightly; *Studio International* (UK), quarterly.

Graphic design
Campaign (UK), weekly; *Communication Arts* (USA), bi-monthly; *Graphis* (Swiss), bi-monthly.

Photography
British Journal of Photography, weekly, *Creative Camera*, monthly.

College courses

Higher Education in the UK. A handbook for students from overseas and their advisers. Longman Group Ltd, for the Association of Commonwealth Universities and British Council.

A Compendium of Advanced Courses in Colleges of Further and Higher Education. London and Home Counties Regional Advisory Council for Technological Education, Tavistock House South, Tavistock Square, London WC1H 9LR.

CNAA Directory of First Degree and Diploma of Higher Education Courses. Council for National Academic Awards, 344–354 Gray's Inn Road, London WC1X 8BP.

Polytechnic Courses Handbook Published by the Committee of Directors of Polytechnics, 309 Regent Street, London W1R 7PE

The Handbook of Degree and Advanced Courses in Institutes, Colleges of Higher Education, Colleges of Education, Polytechnics and University Department of Education. Lund Humphries, The Country Press, Drummond Road, Bradford, BD8 8DH.

4.6 USEFUL ADDRESSES

Suppliers. The following firms are manufacturers, agents, wholesalers or importers of items mentioned in this handbook or of similar items. The majority of local art and design materials stockists in the United Kingdom will be able to supply specific items, but in case of difficulty or when certain specialist items are required it may be necessary to contact the suppliers whose names, addresses and telephone numbers are listed below.

General art and design

Acrylic Paint Company,
28 Thornhill Road, London, N1 1HW.
Tel: 607 0357 (order direct)

Berol Ltd,
Oldmeadow Road, King's Lynn, Norfolk, PE30 4JR.
Tel: 0553 61221

Caran D'Ache,
Jakar International Ltd,
Hillside House, 2–6 Friern Park, London, N12 9BX
Tel: 01 445 6377

A. W. Faber-Castell (UK) Ltd,
Crompton Road, Stevenage, Herts, SG1 2EF
Tel: 0438 66511

Pro Arte,
Sutton-in-Craven, North Yorkshire.
Tel: 0535 32143

Reeves,
Whitefriars Avenue, Wealdstone, Harrow, Middlesex.
Tel: 01 427 4343

Robersons Ltd,
77 Parkway, London, NW1.
Tel: 01 485 1163

Rexel Art & Leisure Products, Ltd,
Gatehouse Road, Aylesbury, Buckinghamshire, HP19 3DT
Tel: 0296 81421

G. Rowney, & Co., Ltd,
PO Box 10, Bracknell, Berkshire, RG12 4ST.
Tel: 0344 24621
(Shop) 12 Percy Street, London, W1A 2BP.
Tel: 01 636 8241

Staedtler (UK) Ltd,
Pontyclun, Mid-Glamorgan, Wales, CF7 8YJ.
Tel: 0443 222421

Winsor & Newton,
Wealdstone, Harrow, HA3 5RH, Middlesex.
Tel: 01 427 4343
(showroom) 51–52 Rathbone Place, London, WLP 1AB

Specialist Suppliers

Boards/papers/sketch-blocks/pads
Barcham Green & Co. Ltd,
Hayle Mill, Maidstone, Kent, ME 15 6XQ.
Tel: 0622 674343

Daler Board Co. Ltd,
Wareham, Dorset.
Tel: 09295 6621

Frisk Ltd,
4 Franthorne Way, Randlesdown Road, London, SE6 3BT.
Tel: 01 698 3481

Marwick & Paulig Ltd,
Legion Works, Kimberley Road, London, NW6.
Tel: 01624 8611

Oram & Robinson, Ltd,
Cadmore Lane, Cheshunt, Waltham Cross, Hertfordshire, EN8
9SG.
Tel: 97 27376

Paper retailers – London
Paper Point (Wiggins Teape Ltd),
63 Poland Street, London, W1.
Tel: 01 439 4414

Paperchase Products Ltd,
213 Tottenham Court Road, London, W1.
Tel: 01 580 8496

Paper suppliers: general.
Robert Hoone Ltd,
(Head Office) Huntsman House, Mansion Close, Moulton Park,
Northampton, NN3 1LA.
Tel: 0604 495 333

Other branches at: Birmingham (Tel: 021 730 1101); Bolton (Tel:
0204 20244); Bristol (Tel: 0272 770799); Cardiff (Tel:
0222 372525); Denny (Tel: 0324 824218); Dublin (Tel: 777081);
Eastleigh (Tel: 0703 618811); Leeds (Tel: 0532 733471); Leicester
(Tel: 0533 714981); London (Tottenham) Tel: 01 801 5511; (F.
Greenfield Ltd) Tel: 01 242 5533; (Tower Bridge) Tel:
01 231 3441; Newcastle (Tel: 0632 584311); Norwich (Tel:
0603 610386); and at Nottingham, Sevenoaks and Slough.

Schoellershammer,
L & W Design Products,
684 Mitcham Road, Croydon, CR9 3AB   ·
Tel: 01 684 6171

Slater Harrison & Co. Ltd,
Lowerhouse Mills, West Bollington, Macclesfield, SK10 5HW.
Tel: 0625 73155
(London Office) 139 St Margarets Road, Twickenham, Middlesex,
TW1 1RG.
Tel: 01 891 0166

Print-making suppliers

L. Cornelissen & Son,
22 Great Queen Street, WC3.
Tel: 01 405 3304

Hunter Penrose Ltd,
7 Spa Road, London, SE16.
Tel: 01 237 6636

T. N. Lawrence & Son Ltd,
Bleeding Hart Yard, Greville Street, Hatton Garden, London, EC1
8SL.
Tel: 01 242 2534

Process Supplies Ltd,
19 Mount Pleasant, London, WC1.
Tel: 01 837 2179

Pronk Davis and Rusby,
90 Brewery Road, London, N7.
Tel: 01 607 4273

Selectasine Serigraphics Ltd,
65 Chislehurst Road, Chislehurst, Kent.
Tel: 01 467 8544
(Shop) 22 Bulstrode Street, London, WLM 5FR.
Tel: 01 935 0768

Sericol Ltd,
26 Parsons Green Lane, London, SW6.
Tel: 01 736 3388

Graphic Design.
C. W. Edding (UK) Ltd,
North Orbital Trading Estate, Napsbury Lane, St Albans, Herts.,
ALI IXQ
Tel: 56 34471

Letraset (UK) Ltd,
195/203, Waterloo Road, London, SE1.
Tel: 01 928 7551

Mecanorma Ltd,
10 School Road, Acton, London, NW10.
Tel: 01 961 6464

Rotobord Ltd,
Stanmore Industrial Estate, Bridgnorth, Shropshire, WV15 5HP
Tel: 07462 4883

Royal Sovereign Graphics,
Britannia House, 100 Drayton Park, London, N5 1NA.
Tel: 226 4455

UNO Sales,
A Division of A. West & Partners Ltd,
684 Mitcham Road, Croydon, CR9 3AB.
Tel: 684 6171

Photography

Kodak Ltd,
(Customer Relations), PO Box 66, Station Road, Hemel
Hempstead, Herts., HP1 1JU.
Tel: 0442 61122

Three-dimensional design

Ceramics
Clayglaze Ltd,
Kings Yard Pottery, Talbot Road, Rickmansworth, Herts.
Tel: Rickmansworth 87107

Wengers Ltd,
Etruria, Stoke-on-Trent, ST4 7BQ.
Tel: 0782 25560

Jewellery/Silversmithing
Silver: Johnson Matthey,
43 Hatton Garden, EC1.
Tel: 01 405 6959

Silversmithing tools: Cooper Bros. & Sons, Ltd,
Mosley House, Holborn Viaduct, London, EC1.
Tel: 01 353 3865

Jewellery tools: Walsh & Gray Ltd,
12–16 Clerkenwell Road, EC1 and 243 Beckenham Road, Kent,
BR3 4TS.
Tel: 01 778 7061

Copper: J. Smith & Sons, Ltd,
50 St John's Square, London, EC1.
Tel: 01 253 1277

Engravers: Guill & Stephenson,
Penny Bank Chambers, St John's Square, EC1.
Tel: 01 250 0651

Plastic: G. H. Bloore Ltd,
480 Honeypot Lane, Stanmore, Middlesex.
Tel: 01 952 2391

Perspex: R. Denny & Co. Ltd,
13–15 Netherwood Road, London, W14.
Tel: 01 603 5152

Stones: C. Calipe,
44 Poland Street, London, W1.
Tel: 01 437 6534

Goldsmiths Hall: Foster Lane, London, EC2.
Tel: 01 606 8971

College addresses

Amersham College of Further Education, Art and Design, Stanley Hill,
   Amersham, HP7 9HN. Tel: Amersham 21121
Barnet College, Wood Street, Barnet, Hertfordshire, EN5 4AZ. Tel:
   01 440 6321.
Barnfield College, New Bedford Road, Luton, LU3 2AX. Tel: Luton
   507531.
Barnsley College of Art and Design, Churchfield, Barnsley, S70 2BH.
   Tel: Barnsley 85623.
Bath Academy of Art, Cosham, Wiltshire, SN13 ODB. Tel: 0249
   712571.
Bath Technical College, Avon Street, Bath, BA1 1UP. Tel: Bath
   312191.
Berkshire College of Art and Design, Raymond Road, Maidenhead,
   SL6 6DF. Tel: Maidenhead 24302.
Birmingham Polytechnic, Admissions Section, Perry Barr, Birmingham,
   B42 2SU. Tel: 021 356 6911.
Blackburn College of Technology and Design, Feilden Street,
   Blackburn, BB2 1LH. Tel: Blackburn 64321
Blackpool and Fylde College of Further and Higher Education,
   Ashfield Road, Bispham, Blackpool, FY2 OHB. Tel: Blackpool
   52352.
Bolton Technical College, Manchester Road, Bolton, BL2 1ER. Tel:
   Bolton 31411.

Boston College of Further Education, Rowley Road, Boston, PE21 6JF. Tel: Boston 65701.

Bournemouth and Poole College of Art and Design, Royal London House, Lansdowne, Bournemouth, BH1 3JL. Tel: Bournemouth 20772.

Bourneville School of Art and Crafts, Lindon Road, Bourneville, Birmingham, B30 1JX. Tel: 021 472 0953.

Bradford College, Great Horton Road, Bradford, West Yorkshire, BD7 1AY. Tel: 0274 34844

Braintree College of Further Education, Church Lane, Braintree, CM7 5SN. Tel: Braintree 21711.

Brighton Polytechnic, Mithras House, Lewes Road, Brighton, BN2 4AT. Tel: 0273 693655.

Bristol Polytechnic, Coldharbour Lane, Frenchay, Bristol, BS16 1QY. Tel: 0272 656261.

Brunel Technical College, Ashley Down, Bristol, BS7 9BU. Tel: Bristol 41241.

Buckinghamshire College of Higher Education, Queen Alexandra Road, High Wycombe, HP11 2JZ. Tel: 0494 22141.

Camberwell School of Art and Crafts, Peckham Road, London, SE5 8UF. Tel: 01 703 0987.

Cambridgeshire College of Arts and Technology, Cambridge, CB1 2AJ. Tel: 0223 63271.

Canterbury College of Art, New Dover Road, Canterbury, CT1 3AN. Tel: 0227 69371.

Cassio College, Langley Road, Watford, WD1 3RH. Tel: Watford 40311.

Caulden College of Further Education, The Concourse, Stoke Road, Shelton, Stoke-on-Trent, ST4 2DG. Tel: 0782 29561

Polytechnic of Central London, 309 Regent Street, London, W1R 8AL. Tel: 01 486 5811.

Central School of Art and Design, Southampton Row, London, WC1B 4AP. Tel: 01 405 1825.

Chelsea School of Art, Manresa Road, London, SW3 6LS. Tel: 01 351 3844.

Chesterfield College of Art and Design, Sheffield Road, Chesterfield, S41 7LL. Tel: Chesterfield 70271.

City and Guilds of London Art School, 124 Kennington Park Road, London, SE11 4DJ. Tel: 01 735 2306.

City of London Polytechnic, Admissions Office, 31 Jewry Street, London, EC3N 2EY. Tel: 01 283 1030.

Cleveland College of Art and Design, Green Lane, Middlesbrough, TS5 7RJ. Tel: Middlesbrough 821441.

Colchester Institute, Sheepen Road, Colchester, CO3 3LL. Tel: 0206 70271.

College for the Distributive Trades, Leicester Square, London, WC2H 7LE. Tel: 01 839 1547.

Cordwainers Technical College, Mare Street, Hackney, London, E8 3RE. Tel: 01 985 0273.

Cornwall Technical College, Redruth, Cornwall, TR15 3RD. Tel: 0209 712911.

Coventry (Lanchester) Polytechnic, Priory Street, Coventry, CV1 5FB. Tel: 0203 57221.

Crewe and Alsager College of Higher Education, Crewe Road, Crewe, CW1 1DU. Tel: 0270 583661.

Croydon College, College Road, Fairfield, Croydon, Surrey, CR9 1DX. Tel: 01 688 9271.

Cumbria College of Art and Design, Brampton Road, Carlisle, CA3 9AY. Tel: Carlisle 25333.

Darlington College of Technology, Cleveland Avenue, Darlington, DL3 7BB. Tel: Darlington 67651.

Dartington College of Arts, Totnes, Devon, T09 6EJ. Tel: 0803 862224.

Derby Lonsdale College of Higher Education, Kedleston Road, Derby, DE3 1GB. Tel: 0332 47181.

Dewsbury and Batley Technical and Art College, Halifax Road, Dewsbury, WF13 2AS. Tel: Dewsbury 465916.

Doncaster Metropolitan Institute of Higher Education, Waterdale, Doncaster, DN1 3EX. Tel: 0302 22122.

Duncan of Jordanstone College of Art, Perth Road, Dundee, DD1 4HT. Tel: 0382 23261.

Dundee College of Technology, Bell Street, Dundee, DD1 1HG. Tel: 0382 23291.

Ealing College of Higher Education, St Mary's Road, Ealing, London, W5 5RF. Tel: 01 579 4111.

East Ham College of Technology, High Street South, London, E6 4ER. Tel: 01 474 1480.

East Warwickshire College of Further Education, Lower Hillmorton Road, Rugby, CV21 3QS. Tel: Rugby 73133.

Epsom School of Art and Design, Ashley Road, Epsom, KT 18 5BE. Tel: Epsom 28811.

Exeter College of Art and Design, Earl Richards Road North, Exeter, EX2 6AS. Tel: 0392 77977.

Falmouth School of Art, Woodlane, Falmouth Cornwall, Tel: 0326 313269.

Farnborough College of Technology, Boundary Road, Farnborough, Hampshire, GU14 6SB. Tel: 0252 515511.

Gateshead Technical College, Durham Road, Gateshead, NE9 5BN. Tel: Gateshead 770524.

Glasgow School of Art, 167 Renfrew Street, Glasgow, G3 6RQ. Tel: 041 332 9797.

Gloucestershire College of Arts and Technology, Pittville, Cheltenham, Gloucestershire, GL52 3JG. Tel: 0242 32501

Goldsmiths' College, New Cross London, SE 14 6NW. Tel: 01 692 0211.

Granville College, Granville Road, Sheffield, S2 2RL. Tel: Sheffield 760271.

Great Yarmouth College of Art and Design, Trafalgar Road, Great Yarmouth, NR 30 2LB. Tel: 0493 3557.

Gwent College of Higher Education, Faculty of Art and Design, Clarence Place, Newport, Gwent, NPT OUW. Tel: 0633 59984.

Harrow College of Higher Education, Watford Road, Northwick Park, Harrow, Middlesex, HA1 3TP. Tel: 01 864 5422.

Havering Technical College, Ardleigh Green Road, Hornchurch, Essex, RM11 211. Tel: Hornchurch 55011.

Harlow Technical College, College Gate, The High, Harlow, CM20 1LT. Tel: Harlow 20131.

Harrogate College of Arts and Adult Studies, 2 Victoria Avenue, Harrogate, HG1 1EL. Tel: Harrogate 62446.

Herefordshire College of Art and Design, Folly Lane, Hereford HR1 1LT. Tel: Hereford 3359.

Hertfordshire College of Art and Design, 7 Hatfield Road, St Albans, AL1 3RS. Tel: St. Albans 64414.

Hounslow Borough College, London Road, Isleworth, Middlesex. Tel: 01 568 0244.

The Polytechnic Huddersfield, Queensgate, Huddersfield, Yorkshire, HD1 3DH. Tel: 0484 22288.

Hull College of Higher Education, Cottingham Road, Hull, HU6 7RT. Tel: 0482 41451.

Ilkley College, Wells Road, Ilkley, West Yorkshire. Tel: 0943 609010.

Isle of Ely College of Further Education and Horticulture, Ramnoth Road, Wisbech, PE13 2JE. Tel: Wisbech 2561.

Jacob Kramer College, Vernon Street, Leeds, LS2 8PH. Tel: Leeds 39931.

Kidderminster College of Further Education, Hoo Road, Kidderminster, DY10 1LX. Tel: 0562 66311.

Kingston Polytechnic, Penrhyn Road, Kingston upon Thames, KT1 2EE. Tel: 01 549 1366.

Kingsway–Princeton College, Sidmouth Street, Grays Inn Road, London, WC1H 8JB. Tel: 01 837 8185.

Kitson College of Technology, Cookridge Street, Leeds, LS2 8BL. Tel: Leeds 30381.

Leeds Polytechnic, Calverley Street, Leeds, LS1 9BH. Tel: 0532 462903.

Leicester Polytechnic, PO Box 143, Leicester, LE1 9BH. Tel: 0533 551551.

Lincolnshire College of Art, Lindum Road, Lincoln, LN2 1NP. Tel: Lincoln 23268.

Liverpool: Central College of Further Education, Clarence Street, Liverpool, L3 5TP. Tel: 051 708 0423.

Liverpool Polytechnic, Rodney House, 70 Mount Pleasant, Liverpool, L3 5UX. Tel: 051 708 6620.

London College of Fashion, 20 John Prince's Street, London, W1M 9HE. Tel: 01 629 9401.

London College of Furniture, 41–71 Commercial Road, London, E1 1LA. Tel: 01 247 1953.

London College of Printing, Elephant and Castle, London, SE1 6SB. Tel: 01 735 8484.

Loughborough College of Art and Design, Radmoor, Loughborough, Leicestershire, LE11 3BT. Tel:0509 61515.

Loughton College of Further Education, Borders Lane, Loughton, IG10 3SA. Tel: 01 508 8311.

Mabel Fletcher Technical College, Sandown Road, Liverpool, L15 4JB. Tel: 051 733 7211.

Maidstone College of Art, Oakwood Park, Oakwood Road, Maidstone, Kent. Tel: 0622 57286.

Manchester Polytechnic, All Saints Buildings, All Saints, Manchester, M15 6BH. Tel: 061 228 6171.

Medway College of Design, Fort Pitt, Rochester, ME1 1DZ. Tel: Medway 44815.

Middlesex Polytechnic, Admissions Office, 114 Chase Side, London, N14 5PN. Tel: 01 886 6599.

Mid-Cheshire College of Further Education, Hartford Campus, Northwich, CW8 1LJ. Tel: Northwich 75281.

Mid-Warwickshire College of Further Education, Warwick New Road, Leamington Spa, CV32 5JE. Tel: Leamington Spa 311711.

Napier College, Colinton Road, Edinburgh EH10 5DT. Tel: 031 447 7070.

Nene College, Moulton Park, Northampton, NN2 7AL. Tel: 0604 715000.

Newcastle upon Tyne College of Arts and Technology, Maple Terrace, Newcastle upon Tyne, NE4 7SA. Tel: Newcastle 738866.

Newcastle upon Tyne Polytechnic, Ellison Building, Ellison Place, Newcastle upon Tyne, NE1 8ST. Tel: 0632 326002

Newcastle under Lyme College of Further Education and School of Art, Liverpool Road, Newcastle, ST5 2DF Tel: Newcastle 611531.

North Devon College, Sticklepath, Barnstaple. Tel: Barnstaple 5291.

North East London Polytechnic, Admissions Enquiry Unit, Asta House, 156 High Road, Chadwell Heath, Romford, Essex, RM6 6LX. Tel: 01 590 7722.

North London Polytechnic, Holloway, London, N7 8DB. Tel: 01 607 2789.

North East Wales Institute of Higher Education, College of Art, Regent Street, Wrexham, LL11 1PF. Tel: Wrexham 365955.

North Staffordshire Polytechnic, College Road, Stoke-on-Trent, ST4 2DE. Tel: 0782 45531.

North Warwickshire College of Technology and Art, Hinckley Road, Nuneaton, CV11 6BH. Tel: Nuneaton 349321.

North Worcestershire College, Bromsgrove, B60 1PQ. Tel: 0527 74151.

Norwich School of Art, St George Street, Norwich, Norfolk, NR3 1BB. Tel: 0603 610 561.

Oxford Polytechnic, Headington, Oxford, OX3 OBP. Tel: 0865 64777.

Paddington College, 25 Paddington Green, London, W2 1NB. Tel: 01 402 6221.

Percival Whitley College of Further Education, Francis Street, Halifax, HX1 3UZ. Tel: Halifax 58221.

Plymouth College of Art and Design, Tavistock Place, Plymouth, P14 8AT. Tel: Plymouth 21312.

Plymouth Polytechnic, Drake Circus, Plymouth, PL4 8AA. Tel: 0752 21312.

Portsmouth College of Art, Design and Further Education, Winston Churchill Avenue, Portsmouth, PO1 2DJ. Tel: Portsmouth 826435.

Portsmouth Polytechnic, Museum Road, Portsmouth, PO1 2QQ. Tel: 0705 27681.

Preston Polytechnic, Educational Liaison Officer, Corporation Street, Preston, PR1 2TQ. Tel: 0772 51831.

Ravensbourne College of Art and Design, Walden Road, Chislehurst, Kent, BR7 5SN. Tel: 01 468 7071.

Redbridge Technical College, Little Heath, Romford, RM6 4XT. Tel: 01 599 5231.

Reigate School of Art and Design, Blackborough Road, Reigate, RH2 7DE. Tel: Redhill 66661.

Richmond upon Thames College, Egerton Road, Twickenham, Middlesex, TW2 7SJ. Tel: 01 892 6656.

Robert Gordon's Institute of Technology, Schoolhill, Aberdeen, AB9 1FR. Tel: 0224 574 511.

Rotherham College of Arts and Technology, Eastwood Lane, Rotherham, S65 IEG. Tel: Rotherham 61801.

Rycotewood College, Priest End, Thame, OX9 2AF. Tel: Thame 2501.

Salford College of Technology, Frederick Road, Salford, M6 6PU. Tel: 061 736 6541.

Salisbury College of Art, Southampton Road, Salisbury, SP1 2LW. Tel: Salisbury 23711.

St Martin's School of Art, 107 Charing Cross Road, London, WC2H ODU. Tel: 01 437 0611.

Scarborough Technical College, Lady Edith's Drive, Scarborough, Y012 5RN. Tel: Scarborough 72105.

Scottish College of Textiles, Netherdale, Galashiels, TD1 3HF. Tel: Galashiels 3351.

Sheffield City Polytechnic, Pond Street, Sheffield, S1 LWB. Tel: 0742 20911.

Solihull College of Technology, Blossomfield Road, Solihull, B91 LSB. Tel: 021 705 6376.

Somerset College of Arts and Technology, Wellington Road, Taunton, TA1 5AX. Tel: Taunton 83403.

Southampton College of Higher Education, East Park Terrace, Southampton, S09 4WW. Tel: 0703 29381.

Polytechnic of the South Bank, Borough Road, London, SE1 0AA. Tel: 01 928 8989.

South Devon Technical College, Newton Road, Torquay, TQ2 5BY. Tel: Torquay 35711.

Southend-on-Sea College of Technology, Carnarvon Road, Southend-on-Sea, SS2 6LS. Tel: Southend-on-Sea 353931.

Southfields College of Further Education, Aylestone Road, Leicester, LE2 7LW. Tel: Leicester 541 818.

Southgate Technical College, High Street, London, N14 6BS. Tel: 01 886 6521.

South Glamorgan Institute of Higher Education, Faculty of Art and Design, Howard Gardens, Cardiff, CF2 1SP. Tel: 0222 482 202.

South Shields Marine and Technical College, St George's Avenue, South Shields, NE 34 6ET. Tel: South Shields 560. 403.

South Thames College, Wandsworth High Street, London, SW 18 2PP. Tel: 01 870 2241.

Southwark College, The Cut, London, SE1 8LE. Tel: 01 928 9561.

Stafford College of Further Education, Earl Street, Stafford, ST16 2QR. Tel: Stafford 42361.

Stevenage College, Monkswood Way, Stevenage, SG1 1LA. Tel: Stevenage 2822.

Stockport College of Technology, Wellington Road South, Stockport, SK1 3UQ. Tel: 061 480 7331.

Stourbridge College of Technology and Art, Church Street, Stourbridge, West Midlands. Tel: 038 437 8531.

Suffolk College of Higher and Further Education, Rope Walk, Ipswich, 1P4 1LT. Tel: Ipswich 55885.

Sunderland Polytechnic, Langham Tower, Ryhope Road, Sunderland, SR2 7EE. Tel: 0783 76233.

Sutton Coldfield College of Further Education, Lichfield Road, Sutton Coldfield, B74 2NW. Tel: 021 355 5671.

Swindon: The College, Regent Circus, Swindon, SN1 1PT. Tel: Swindon 40131.

Tameside College of Technology, Beaufort Road, Ashton-under-Lyne, 0L6 6NX. Tel: 061 330 6911.

Teesside Polytechnic, Middlesbrough, Cleveland, TS1 3BA. Tel: 0642 218121.

Thames Polytechnic, Wellington Street, Woolwich, London, SE18 6PF. Tel: 01 854 2030.

Thurrock Technical College, Woodview, Grays, Essex, RM16 4YR. Tel: Grays Thurrock 71621.

Trent Polytechnic, Burton Street, Nottingham, NG1 4BU. Tel: 0602 48248.

Trowbridge Technical College, College Road, Trowbridge, BA14 OES. Tel: Trowbridge 66241.

Ulster Polytechnic, Shore Road, Newtownabbey, Co. Antrim,
   Northern Ireland, BT37 0QB. Tel: 1231 65131.
Uxbridge Technical College, Park Road, Uxbridge, Middlesex, UB8
   1NQ. Tel: Uxbridge 30411.
Wakefield District College, Margaret Street, Wakefield, WF1 2DH.
   Tel: Wakefield 70501.
Watford College, School of Art and Design, Ridge Street, Watford.
   Tel: 92 26816
Ware College, Scotts Road, Ware, SG12 9JF. Tel: Ware 5441.
West Bromwich College of Commerce and Technology, Woden Road
   South Wednesbury, West Midlands, WS10 0PE. Tel: 021 569
   4656.
West Glamorgan Institute of Higher Education, Townhill Road,
   Townhill, Swansea, SA2 OUT. Tel: Swansea 23482.
West Midlands College of Higher Education, Gorway, Walsall, West
   Midlands, WS1 3BD. Tel: 0922 29141.
West Nottinghamshire College of Further Education, Derby Road,
   Mansfield, NG18 5BH. Tel: Mansfield 27191.
West Surrey College of Art and Design, Falkner Road, The Hart,
   Farnham, Surrey, GU9 7DS. Tel: 0252 722441.
West Sussex College of Design, Union Place, Worthing, BN11 1LQ.
   Tel: Worthing 31116.
Wigan College of Technology, Parsons Walk, Wigan, WN1 1RR. Tel:
   0942 494911.
Willesden College of Technology, Denzil Road, London, NW10 2XD.
   Tel: 01 451 3411.
Wimbledon School of Art, Merton Hall Road, Wimbledon, London,
   SW19 3QA Tel: 01 540 0231.
Winchester School of Art, Park Avenue, Winchester, Hampshire, S023
   8DL. Tel: 0962 61891.
Wirral College of Art, Design and Adult Studies, Withens Lane.
   Wallasey, L45 7LT. Tel: 051 639 1268.
Wolverhampton Polytechnic, Molineux Street, Wolverhampton, WV1
   1SB. Tel: 0902 710 654.
Worcester Technical College, Deansway, Worcester, WR1 2JF. Tel:
   Worcester 28383.
W. R. Tuson College, St Vincent's Road, Fulwood, Preston, PR2
   4UR. Tel: Preston 716511.
York College of Arts and Technology, Dringhouses, York, YO2 1UA.
   Tel: York 704141.

Professional Institutes and associations, academic bodies, art and design organisations and other related areas

Art and Design Admissions Registry (ADAR),
Imperial Chambers, 24 Widemarsh Street, Hereford, HR4 9EO
   (written enquiries only).

Association of Illustrators,
17 Carlton House Terrace, London, S.W.1.
Tel: 01 930 5071

Business and Technician Education Council (DATEC),
Central House, Upper Woburn Place, London, WC1H OHH.
Tel: 01 388 3288

British Display Society,
24 Ormond Road, Richmond, Surrey, TW10 6TH.
Tel: 01 948 4151

British Institute of Interior Design,
22–24 South Street, Ilkeston, Derbyshire.
Tel: 0602 329781

City and Guilds of London Institute,
76 Portland Place, London, W1N 4AA.
Tel: 01 580 3050

The Clothing Institute,
Albert Road, Hendon, London, NW4.
Tel: 01 203 0191

Council for National Academic Awards (CNAA),
344–354 Gray's Inn Road, London, WC1X 8BP

Crafts Council,
12 Waterloo Place, Lower Regent Street, London, SW1Y 4AU.
Tel: 01 930 4811

Department of Education and Science (DES),
Elizabeth House, 39 York Road, London SE1 7PH.
Tel: 01 928 9222

Department of Education for Northern Ireland,
Rathgael House, Balloo Road, Bangor, Co. Down, BT19 2PR.
Tel: Bangor 66311

Design Council,
28 Haymarket, London, SW1Y 4SU.
Tel: 01 839 8000

Design Council,
72 Vincent Street, Glasgow G2 5TN.
Tel: 041 221 1621

Institute of Incorporated Photographers (IIP),
2 Amwell End, Ware, Hertfordshire, SG12 9HN.
Tel: 0920 4011

Institute of Packaging,
Fountain House, 1A Elm Park, Stanmore, HA7 4BZ.
Tel: 01 954 6277

Scottish Education Department, New St James House, St James
Centre, Edinburgh, EH1 3SY.
Tel: 031 556 8400

Society of Industrial Artists and Designers (SIAD),
12 Carlton House Terrace, London, SW1Y 5AH.
Tel: 01 930 1911

Textile Institute,
10 Blackfriars Street, Manchester, M3 5DR.
Tel: 061 834 1457

Universities' Central Council on Admissions (UCCA),
PO Box 28, Cheltenham, Gloucestershire. G150 1HY
Tel: 0242 59091

Index